CINDY ZLOTNIK ORAVECZ

Flowers in a Flash

Bias Outline Appliqué

Dedication

This book is dedicated to all stitchers that every day share a kind word, a helpful hint, a complaint, a worry, a tear or any other slice of life with each other. Together, we create this big beautiful invisible quilt of our shared lives through this wonderful medium we love – creating with our hands and the common thread.

Acknowledgments

Many thanks to the people who generously supported the production of this book with their great talents, time and friendships.

Editors: Stephen Oravecz, Peg Viole
Graphic Designer: Lynda Smith
Photographers: Stephen Oravecz, Joe Rudenic
Administrative Assistant: Renee Hoffstetter of Quilter's Fancy
Artistic Consultant: Julia Oravecz
Sewing Support: Susan Naughton, Peg Viole of Designers Two
Product Support: Clover Needlecraft Inc., Martelli Enterprises,
The Warm Company, Northcott Monarch Fabrics,
J.T. Trading Company, Sulky of America, YLI Corp

Flowers In A Flash: Bias Outline Appliqué

First Printing, First Edition
Copyright 2006 Cindy Zlotnik Oravecz
Published by Quilter's Fancy, P.O. Box 457, Cortland, Ohio 44410-1129 U.S.A.

ISBN 0-9652160-3-9

Contents

Introduction

Open the pages of this book and open up your creativity to a very fast, easy and rewarding way to put together a colorful masterpiece – outline appliqué with Clover Needlecraft's Mini Bias.

Blend these nine whimsical flower vases into a wallhanging where each vase of flowers "cozies up" to neighboring flower vases causing a playful riot of color.

Choose to set these flower vases into a more traditional block setting in a full-size quilt. But look closely at the Rainbow Album Quilt and notice half quilt blocks filled with single flowers. These half blocks stagger the setting of the blocks for a new and refreshing way to put blocks together!

A small wallhanging of the Stained Glass Hearts can be sewn, quilted and bound in just 3 hours. That's a fast wallhanging.

The magic is in a fusible bias that is just ⅛ inch wide. By simply holding the thin bias strip of fabric in one hand and the Clover Mini Iron in the other, and pressing the bias along the raw edge of fused fabric, and ironing it in place,

beautiful finished motifs are made instantly. Machine sew the bias in place with a twin needle and tuck raw edges of Mini Bias under other pieces of fabric using the Clover Tapered Awl.

Clover Mini Bias is perfectly made so it is uniform in size. The fusing behind this 100 percent cotton bias is of the highest quality. If Clover Mini Bias is ironed down in the wrong place, merely peel it up and iron it down again. Bias is very forgiving!

The Rainbow Album has a technique that makes the colors zing. The magic is all in the way that Rainbow Mini Bias interacts with the brilliant hues of fabrics. Making colors zing is so simple to do.

Whimsical big daisies from the Rainbow Sampler can be used to make very fun and very fast hot pads and potholders for the kitchen. The bright and happy flowers just shout happiness wherever you place them. From towels to curtains or on the edge of a jacket or on a quilt these big daisies will dance.

The designs used in the Rainbow Album share common templates so there are not so many shapes to trace and use.

Lite Steam-A-Seam 2 has become my non-woven fusible web of choice for one main reason – it keeps fused fabric designs soft, not stiff. Also when the shape is cut out and paper removed, Lite Steam-A-Seam 2 has a slightly sticky surface. This makes it easy to position before ironing it in place. It will stick temporarily in place before it is ironed in place permanently allowing repositioning of pattern pieces if necessary.

If you can drive your car down the road, you can successfully sew down fusible bias. Sewing with a twin needle is just as easy as sewing with a single needle. Just drive those twin needles right down the road of fusible bias.

Bonus patterns of Sliced Pickles, Stained Glass Hearts, Stained Glass Pine Trees and Castle Window are included in this book. Clover's ¼-inch Quick Bias is applied in continuous lines for more easy fun.

> Here are the two basic principles of this technique:
> - *Use ⅛-inch wide mini bias to outline and cover raw edges of a fused fabric shape.*
> - *Use ¼-wide quick bias to cover where the raw edges of two pieces meet.*

Pre-made shirred bias strips are available now in Clover's Flower Chenille Brooch Kit. When paired up with Clover's ¼-inch Quick Bias, create a fantastic textured purse fast. The possibilities for creating with this shirred bias are boundless.

Pick your favorite color scheme and grab your Clover Mini Iron and some fusible Mini Bias and let's outline applique some bright, happy flowers – quick!

Happy Stitching,
Cindy Oravecz

Things To Know Before Beginning

Fabric – Choose fabrics in rainbow colors of yellow, orange, red, magenta, light purple, blue and green. Colors that are mottled blends of light, medium and dark tones all in one fabric work well. Study the color photos for fabric ideas.

Prewash fabric? – Always prewash the cotton background fabric for quilt blocks. For the Rainbow Album, prewash background fabric and cut 17-inch squares. If background fabric is not prewashed, this fabric could shrink anywhere from ¼ inch to a ½ inch. Background blocks need to be squared up to 16½ inches when all sewing and pressing is completed so the finished quilt will hang evenly.

Snippet Bag — Use a gallon size, clear zippered plastic bag to keep all the snippets of Rainbow Mini Bias accumulated while working. Put all pieces in the bag regardless of how small. When fussy cutting the Mini Bias, glance into the bag and quickly reach for the color needed.

Mistakes? — I make mistakes all the time. Do you? I wish I could place every fabric piece perfectly every time. But boy, do I make mistakes and want to change things in hindsight! That's why here's the best secret about Lite Steam-A-Seam 2. After fusing fabric pieces to the background block, these pieces can be repositioned. Work a scissor point under the applique piece. Then peel it up, reposition and re-iron. Clover Mini Bias also can be repositioned and re-ironed. It continues to stick in place. I just love techniques like this that let you make mistakes and fix them with no trouble.

Organizing Paper Pieces – Clear page protectors are excellent ways to keep paper pieces from each design together and laying flat during the paper cutting stage and fusing stage. Otherwise, one brisk breeze can blow cut paper pieces all over.

Loosening the fused paper from the fabric – Sometimes the paper adheres very closely to the fabric depending on how much heat has been applied. First, crease the piece to loosen the paper. If this does not work, take a pin and slide it in between the paper and the fabric to loosen the paper.

Laying Tool for Machine Sewing – A good laying tool for holding bias corners and points flat under the presser foot when machine sewing is an important aid. The Clover Tapered Awl with a very sharp point and the Sew Mate® from Martelli Enterprises with two different edges are both excellent tools for smoothing corners and points of Mini Bias flat when machine sewing. One of the edges on Sew Mate® is 3/16 inch wide and flat. With the presser foot in the down position, this tool can slide under the presser foot to hold mitered corners and pleats in place.

Which Presser Foot To Use?

When sewing bias with a twin needle, use the regular presser foot on the sewing machine. The open toe foot is not recommended as the bias will not lie flat.

Pressing Wood Block – Sometimes Mini Bias may not fuse as well to fabric that has sizing on it. In this case, use a regular size iron to apply heat to a large area of a design. After lifting the iron, immediately lay a wood pressing block on top of the area. Allow the fabric to cool while pressing down on the wood block. The wood pressing block provides superior pressing.

Clover Mini Iron Safety – Keep the Clover Mini Iron at the lower right side of the work surface if right handed. Keep the iron at the lower left side of the work surface if left handed. This keeps the iron cord from getting in the way. Keep rolls of Mini Bias and lengths of Mini Bias at the top of the work surface so that these two supplies do not get tangled while working.

Combine the flower center from Tansy & Coneflower Duet (page 29), the daisy petals from Dancing Daisies (page 66), and leaves from Lacey Petticoats (page 47), to create a lovely single daisy.

Spray Adhesive Basting – To prevent any possible shifting of the layers of the quilt or wallhanging, spray temporary fabric adhesive on the batting.

Fussy Cutting Fabric Pieces – Gradation of color within each pattern piece is important when making flowers and leaves especially. Seek variegated fabric for this reason. When cutting a petal or a leaf, capture areas of the fabric that go from dark to medium to light. Lay a paper piece on the right side first to see exactly where to cut. Then take two or more Clover Flower Head pins and poke the pins straight into the fabric down into the ironing board around the piece as shown in the photo below.

Then flip the fabric, peel off the paper from the paper piece and stick the piece onto the back of the fabric exactly where the pins are

positioned as in photo on right. Iron the piece in place and remove the pins. This method gives exact fussy cutting of pattern pieces as in shown in the photo below.

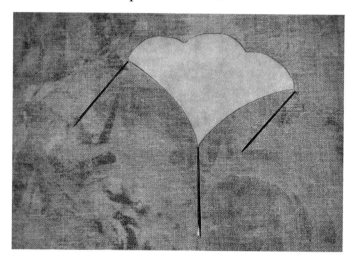

Batik fabric that has mixed colors that shade from light to dark are perfect for capturing dramatic color changes in flowers. The Poppy pictured below from the Poppy Panache Block on the Rainbow Album Wallhanging has deep dark orange at the bottom radiating into lighter orange at top scalloped edges. Try to capture the same color gradation in all the flowers in one block for color repetition.

Fussy Cutting Rainbow Mini Bias – Fussy cutting means particular colors in the fabric or the Clover Mini Bias are specially cut out to fit into a pattern. Stems are fussy cut from Rainbow Mini Bias and may vary in length depending on placement of flower heads. Lay vase and flower heads in place, then audition how a certain color of the Clover Rainbow Mini Bias will look for the stem. Cut the length of bias needed leaving ⅜ inch at each end to tuck under other pieces.

Vase Placement – Make sure the bottom edge of each vase lies exactly parallel to the bottom raw edge of the background block. This will insure that the design sits squarely on each block. For wallhanging, make sure the bottom edge of all three vases in each row lie on the same imaginary horizontal line.

Why the Clover Mini Iron and not an iron with a larger sole plate? – Very few larger irons send heat to the very tip of the iron. The entire 1⅜-inch head of the Clover Mini Iron gets hot. It is the very tip of this hot mini iron that is exactly what is needed to fuse Mini Bias. It is the most suitable tool for the job. It is easier to fuse Mini Bias in straight lines and to make dramatic bias curves when fusing with the Clover Mini Iron as well. Using a larger iron can result in wavy Mini Bias lines where straight ones are desired.

Mitering can be imprecise and raw edges of fabric can not be covered by bias because its just hard to see over the larger iron.

Mitering Points – The Clover Mini Iron & Awl can be used to miter points. Use the tip of the Clover awl to hold bias about 1/16 inch past where the pleat or miter will be as in top photo. Carefully slide the Clover Mini Bias over the point of the awl and press pleat with the Clover Mini Iron as in bottom photo.

Whoops! What if the raw edge of the fabric piece does not get trapped under the twin needle stitching and the Mini Bias? – First poke a straight pin at each end of the stitching that is not catching the fabric. Turn the area to the back side. This is how the section to be removed can be defined. Take a sharp seam ripper and run it up the zigzag stitching channel between the two pins. Remove excess thread from Mini Bias on front. Re-stitch the area back tacking at the beginning and ending of the area. Try to line the needles up with the holes that were left from the first stitching. The repair will be undetectable.

Placement of Quilt Block Pieces – Always place the most outer edge of the pieces of the design three inches from the raw edge of a 17-inch quilt block. Blocks will be squared up to 16½ inches when all sewing is completed. Blocks will be 16 inches square when sewn together in the finished quilt.

Placement of Wallhanging Pieces on One Yard Background – All nine blocks blend together with ½ inch spacing between flowers of neighboring blocks. Flowers of each block nestle closely together. Leave a 2½-inch allowance around the nine-blocks to the raw edge for background fabric.

Special Sewing Order – When flowers sit close together in the design, sew the Mini Bias on these petals down first. Give the background fabric an extra smoothing out with your hands. This will prevent any bunching up of the background fabric between flowers.

Know the names/sizes of Clover Bias
Clover bias comes in a multitude of colors. See Books, Tools & Supplies, page 96.
Sizes to know:
• Miniature Bias is ⅛-inch wide
• Clover Quick Bias is ¼-inch wide
• Clover Border Bias is ¾-inch wide
• Gathered bias strip is part of the Flower Chenille Brooch Kit
• The French company Bohin has a ¼-inch wide bias in variegated soft taupe colors and rainbow colors.

A Coneflower from Tansy & Coneflower Duet (page 29) along with leaves from Poppy Panache (page 55) were used in a half block in the Rainbow Album Quilt.

Making Colors Zing

Rainbow Mini Bias can do the ultimate tango with brightly colored bali fabrics. A tango is a dance so spellbinding to the dancers and to those watching that it is absolutely delightful to watch every move.

The tango between Rainbow Mini Bias and bali fabrics can be so spellbinding that it is fun to gaze upon the colors interacting.

First, let's choose a dramatic background. For brightly colored Bali fabrics, a dark neutral is the answer. Perhaps black fabric is the best answer but other dark neutrals like green, navy or purple can work as well.

Let's take a black background and pepper it with a small quiet print to give it some interest. Take a look at the background fabric used in the Rainbow Album Quilt.

Northcott Fabrics brings us a black fabric with an all-over gold print called Heavy Metal. Both the black and gold form a neutral background to allow the Bali colors and Rainbow Mini Bias to steal the show.

In the wallhanging, the dark dramatic background was navy with a fine line, multi-color scribble print.

If you like looking at these quilt block patterns, it is necessary to learn why. It is fun to look at these flower vases because of the way the colors come together.

The secret to color placement could not be easier – *place like colors together.* In addition, place neighboring colors on the color wheel, also known as analogous colors, right next to each other.

Notice the green leaves throughout these quilt blocks. The leaves are mostly surrounded by green Mini Bias. But there also are areas where bits of blue green surround leaves and bits of yellow green surround leaves.

Don't match too much! Allow these interesting neighboring colors to pop in on the traditional or expected colors.

Bluebells are surrounded by mostly blue mini bias. However, there are spots where purple and green – two colors that neighbor blue — are peeking into the picture.

Take a look at the yellow coneflower on the book cover. The petals are yellow and the section of Rainbow Mini Bias that surrounds each petal is yellow. On the Clover Rainbow Mini Bias as on the color wheel, yellow shifts into yellow green. Yellow and yellow green are neighboring colors on the color wheel and on Rainbow Mini Bias. I allowed a bit of yellow green to border the yellow petals of the coneflower. In fact, allowing a bit of yellow green to break up all yellow petals adds interest to the colors and allows the colors to zing.

Sometimes, you may not find the exact color in Rainbow Mini Bias to surround a Bali fabric.

Take a look at the Stately Tulips block. The tulips are a vibrant magenta – a deeper pink color. The colors in Rainbow Mini Bias move from orange to red to purple. There is no magenta or pink in the Rainbow Mini Bias.

But pink and red are neighboring colors on the color wheel. In other words, pink blends into red. So when I surrounded my magenta-colored tulips with red mini bias, the colors were quite pleasant together. In fact, the colors zinged because we dared to push the two neighboring colors together.

It is that color zing that captures our attention. Place that zing on the dramatic dark or black neutral background, and you will have a color winner of a quilt – a quilt that people can't take their eyes off of.

Rainbow Album

Wallhanging 45" x 56"

Fabric & Thread Needed To Create
The Rainbow Album Quilt (finished size 64" x 80")

1 yard of background fabric
2 yards of border fabric
5 yards of backing fabric
½ yard each of the following variegated fabrics:
yellow, orange, red, magenta, purple, blue, green
5 (11-yard) spools of Clover Rainbow Mini Bias
2 (11-yard) spools of Clover Black Mini Bias
1¼ spool (8½ yards) of Clover Rainbow Border Bias for binding if desired
2 spools of clear monofilament thread
Cotton-covered polyester thread for bobbin that matches backing fabric
5 yards Lite Steam-A-Seam 2® double stick fusible web

Tools Needed

Clover Mini Iron
The Sew-Mate® from Martelli Enterprises
Clover Tapered Tailor's Awl
Schmetz Twin Needles size 2.5 (fits all sewing machines)
Clover Flower Head Pins
Scissors for cutting paper
Scissors for cutting fabric
A clear plastic page protector
505 Spray And Fix™ or Sulky KK2000™ temporary spray adhesive
One zippered plastic bag to hold cut pieces of Clover Mini Bias
A 20-inch square rotary ruler for squaring blocks
Template plastic
Sewing machine

Fabric & Thread Needed To Create
The Rainbow Album Wallhanging
(finished size 45" x 56")

1 yard of background fabric
2 yards of border fabric
2 yards of backing fabric
½ yard each of the following variegated fabrics:
yellow, orange, red, magenta, purple, blue, green
4 (11-yard) spools of Clover Rainbow Mini Bias
1 (11-yard) spool of Clover Black Mini Bias
1 spool (6 yards) of Clover Rainbow Border Bias for binding if desired
2 spools of clear monofilament thread
Cotton-covered polyester thread for bobbin that matches backing fabric
4 yards Lite Steam-A-Seam 2® double stick fusible web

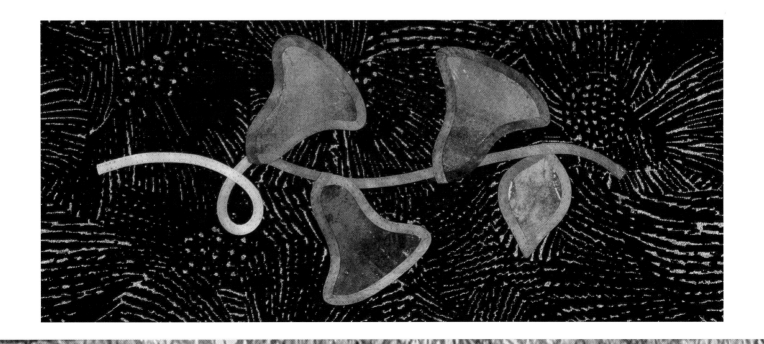

The Basic Technique

1 Choose shapes needed and cut out of template plastic.

2 Trace the quantity of each shape needed onto one side of Lite Steam-A-Seam 2.

3 Cut shapes out carefully on pencil line using a quality pair of scissors for cutting paper.

4 Peel off one side of paper.

5 Stick Lite Steam-A-Seam 2 template on fabric. It will temporarily stick in place.

6 Press Lite Steam-A-Seam 2 template in place on wrong side of fabric for about 6 seconds.

7 Cut Lite Steam-A-Seam 2 and fabric together on traced line. Remove paper.

8 Position fabric shape in place on background fabric. Smooth fabric piece in place and it will stick. This piece can be picked up and rearranged as needed. This is the most convenient part of Steam-A-Seam 2 Lite.

9 Press pieces for 10-15 seconds with a medium/high heat iron to permanently bond fusing.

10 Press ⅛-inch wide Clover Mini Bias around the shape covering raw edges.

11 If making a top that will be quilted later twin needle sew with matching or clear thread over Mini Bias.

12 Layer batting and backing under block or wallhanging. Apply spray adhesive between block, batting and backing, smoothing all layers carefully.

13 If twin needle sewing and quilting the project in one step, sew over Mini Bias through batting and backing.

Creating The Rainbow Album

Needles and Thread Needed:

• Two Schmetz 2.5/80 Twin Needles, always stock a spare twin needle

• Clear YLI Wonder Invisible or Sew Art International monofilament thread

> *NOTE: All suggested colors that follow are for creating the Rainbow Album from brightly colored fabrics but choose any colors desired for different looks.*

For each block, prepare pattern pieces in the following way:

1. Trace all pieces in pencil onto Lite Steam-A-Seam 2.

2. Cut all pieces out carefully and neatly on pencil line.

3. Peel one side of paper off each piece.

4. Place piece onto the wrong side of fabric. Press lightly.

5. Cut each piece out, cutting exactly around the edge of each piece carefully.

6. Place pieces onto background fabric and lay out in an approximate placement before peeling off the final paper and sticking in place.

7. Peel paper off pieces and stick onto background fabric. Smooth pieces in place. Pieces can still be moved and rearranged.

8. When pieces are in place to your liking, press in place.

Threading the Twin Needle:

Threading a Twin Needle is just like threading your sewing machine with a standard machine needle with these exceptions:

1. Place one spool of invisible monofilament thread on the right spool holder. Immediately thread the monofilament through *the extra threading loop* that is often on the back of the sewing machine or the back of the sewing machine handle depending on model.

> *NOTE: If there is not an extra threading loop near the spool holder, tape a safety pin near the spool holder and run the thread through the circular end of the safety pin. This is an instant extra loop threader wherever needed.*

2. When approaching the tension disk, keep this right spool thread to the right of the tension disk. Continue threading the machine as usual.

3. When approaching the twin needle, thread this right spool thread into the right hand needle.

4. Repeat the above for the left spool thread. Share the exact threading pathway as the right spool thread except take the thread to the left at the tension disk and into the left twin needle.

5. Sew as with a single needle with this exception:

<ins>It is impossible to needle down and pivot with a twin needle.</ins>

When pivoting, lift the presser foot and needle up and carefully turn the work. Bring the needle as close to the last stitch as possible. Do not lift the presser foot to its highest position when pivoting. Instead, lift the presser foot just enough so it hugs the fabric when pivoting. This way the thread does not get too much slack in it before taking the next stitch.

NOTE: When machine sewing over many layers of Mini Bias and fabric move the machine hand wheel manually so as not to bend or break a needle.

Threading the Bobbin: Choose thread that matches the backing fabric. Some sewing machines have a threading finger on the bobbin. Thread this extra finger in the bobbin in order to prevent the bobbin thread from poking up through the stitches into the monofilament stitch. If using a sewing machine that does not have this threading finger on the bobbin, loosen needle tension on the sewing machine. If thread still wants to pop up through stitches on the front of the work, loosen the bobbin tension.

HELPFUL HINT: Some residue can collect on the twin needles from sewing through Lite-Steam-a-Seam 2 and bias. Watch if stitch quality changes or the machine seems to be laboring and making an unusual sound. Remove the needle from the machine. Carefully clean the needle with an alcohol saturated cottonball periodically.

Dazzling Dahlias

This design is the same for the wallhanging or the quilt except for the small leaf on the quilt block.

Fabric and Clover Mini Bias Needed:

Cut one Vase Center from teal green fabric

Cut one Vase from red or blue fabric

Cut two Stems from Rainbow Clover Mini Bias

Cut one large Dahlia Center from purple fabric

Cut one small Dahlia Center from purple fabric

Cut eight small Dahlia Petals from pink fabric

Cut 11 large Dahlia Petals from
    magenta-orange mix fabric

Cut one Small Leaf from green fabric

Five yards of Clover Rainbow Mini Bias
    for Wallhanging or Quilt

**Press pieces in place
and sew in this order:**

1 – Vase

2 – Stems

3 – Dahlia Petals

4 – Dahlia Centers

5 – Leaves

COLOR HINT: *Fussy cut all the petals* __*the same way*__ *so color gradates from deep dark magenta on one end of the petal and fades into brighter orange toward the other end of each petal.*

Placement of Dazzling Dahlias

1. Peel paper from the back of all the pieces.

2. Place the bottom raw edge of the Vase 3 inches up from the bottom edge of the 17-inch square background block centered. Next place Vase Center on top of vase.

3. Place large Dahlia Center 1¾ inches up from Vase Center top edge. The right edge of the Dahlia Center should be 1⅛ inch from the vertical center of the quilt block.

4. Place the 11 Large Dahlia Petals around this circle so that petal tips just touch circle. Leave ¼ inch of space between each petal and all 11 petals will fit neatly and evenly around the circle.

5. The Mini Bias stem for this Large Dahlia radiates from the Dahlia Center between two petals and curves downward into the vase at the horizontal halfway point of the Vase Center.

6. Place the Small Dahlia Center about 4¼ inches to the right of the edge of the Large Dahlia Center.

7. Place small Dahlia Petals so that each petal tip touches the edge of the Dahlia Center and so there is ¼ inch of space between petals. Keep petal outer edges about 2¼ inches in from quilt block edge.

8. Mini Bias stem also fits between two petals and curves downward into

Vase. The stems at the Vase are about 1¼ inch apart.

9. Place small Leaf at the bottom of smaller Dahlia stem to fill space between petals.

Fusing Clover Mini Bias to Dazzling Dahlias

1. Fuse Mini Bias around Vase Center and Vase first. On this design, the Large Dahlia Petals overlap onto the Vase Center and Vase. While fusing the Mini Bias, use the Clover Awl to peel up the two Large Dahlia Petals that overlap onto the Vase Center. Slide the Mini Bias under the petals. Petals can be ironed down again and will fuse in place over the Mini Bias.

Color Hint: It is surprising how the Rainbow colors of Mini Bias interact with other flower colors. For flower colors, fussy cut and fuse red Mini Bias around the pink petals.

2. For both flowers, starting at the Dahlia Center, fuse Mini Bias around one petal mitering at petal outer tip. Start and end the Mini Bias at the raw edge of the Dahlia Center for each petal.

3. *For both flowers the Mini Bias will be applied last around Dahlia Center after all the petals are sewed down with a*

twin needle. This way the petals can be sewed continuously without having to stop and start stitching after each petal.

4. To fuse Mini Bias to Dahlia center bring ending raw edge of bias ¼-inch past the beginning raw edge. Cut this tail on a diagonal. Fold and crease in the shape this tail will tuck under. Loosen Mini Bias with awl. Tuck folded end under Mini Bias to form a round Dahlia Center.

HINT: The tucked under edge on the Dahlia center may look bulky but when sewn down with the twin needle, the center will flatten down and smooth out into a round circle.

Sewing Mini Bias To Dazzling Dahlias

1. Sew around Vase and Vase Center.

2. Follow arrows and sew bias around petals for both flowers.

Note: While sewing around the Dahlia Centers lift the presser foot every couple of stitches. Do not drag and pull around the curves.

3. Start sewing around the Dahlia Center where it meets the stem. Continue stitching down the stem.

Placement of the Dazzling Dahlias is the same for both the wallhanging and the full-size quilt, except for a small leaf on the quilt block.

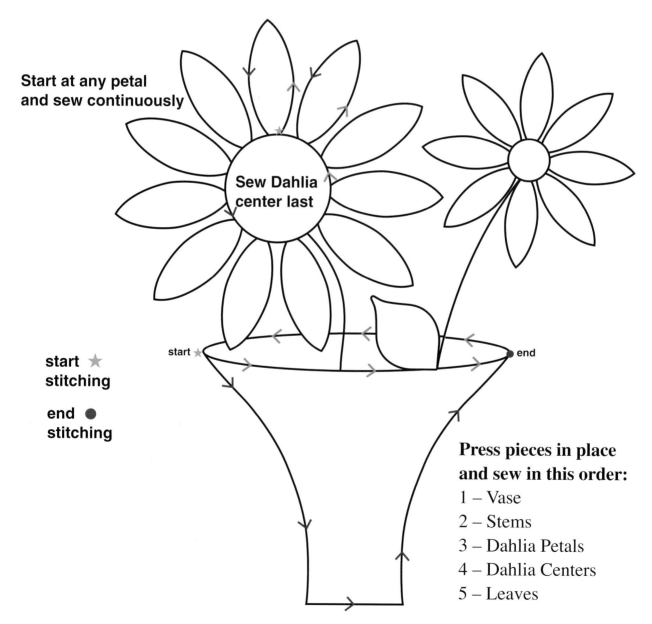

Start at any petal and sew continuously

Sew Dahlia center last

start ★

start ★
stitching

end ●
stitching

end ●

Press pieces in place and sew in this order:
1 – Vase
2 – Stems
3 – Dahlia Petals
4 – Dahlia Centers
5 – Leaves

Placement & Stitching Diagram

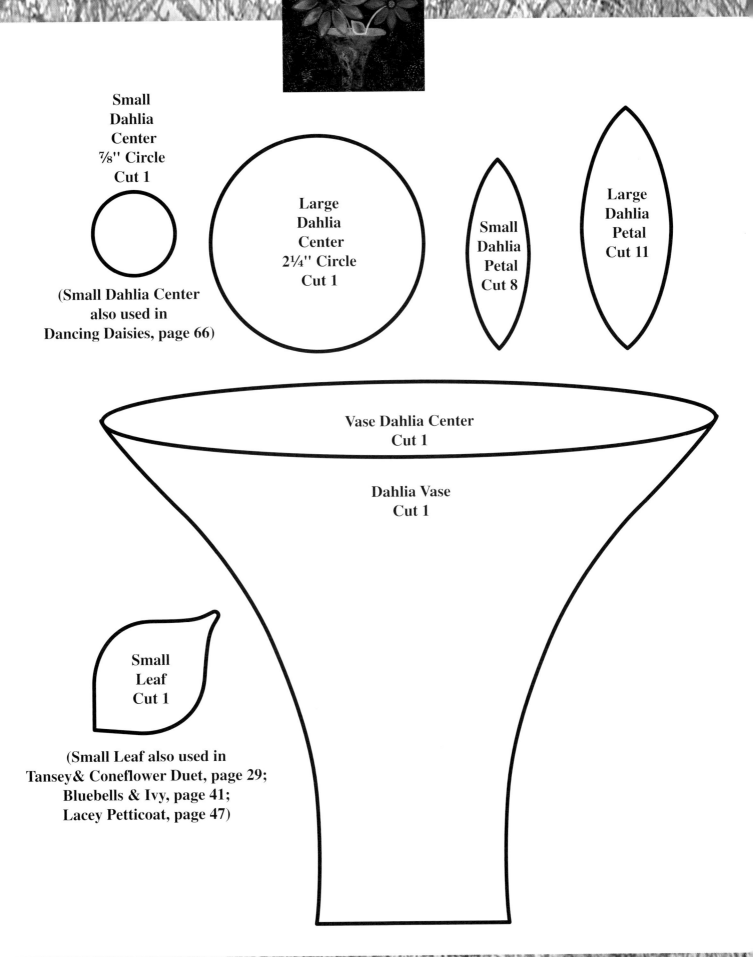

Small
Dahlia
Center
⅞" Circle
Cut 1

(Small Dahlia Center
also used in
Dancing Daisies, page 66)

Large
Dahlia
Center
2¼" Circle
Cut 1

Small
Dahlia
Petal
Cut 8

Large
Dahlia
Petal
Cut 11

Vase Dahlia Center
Cut 1

Dahlia Vase
Cut 1

Small
Leaf
Cut 1

(Small Leaf also used in
Tansey & Coneflower Duet, page 29;
Bluebells & Ivy, page 41;
Lacey Petticoat, page 47)

Tansy & Coneflower Duet

This design is exactly the same for the wallhanging or the quilt.

Fabric and Clover Mini Bias Needed:	Press pieces in place and sew in this order:

Cut one Vase Center from purple fabric
Cut one Vase from magenta fabric
Cut four Stems from Rainbow Clover Mini Bias
Cut five Leaves from green fabric
Cut nine Coneflower Petals from blue-green fabric
Cut one Coneflower Center from blue fabric
Cut two Tansy Tops, one from red fabric,
   one from orange fabric
Cut two Tansy Bottoms, one from red fabric,
   one from orange fabric
4¼ yards of Rainbow Clover Mini Bias
	1 – Vase
	2 – Stems
	3 – Leaves
	4 – Flowers

Placement of Tansy & Coneflower Duet

1. Peel paper from the back of all the pieces.

2. Place the bottom raw edge of the Vase 3 inches up from the bottom edge of the 17-inch square background block centered. Next place Vase Center on top of vase.

3. To figure the placement of all other pieces, make a chalk mark at the center of Vase. Place the two center stems each ⅜ inch to the right and left of the chalk mark respectively.

4. Notice leaves fill the empty space between the petals of neighboring flowers.

5. Outer Coneflower edges are three inches from raw edge of 17-inch square background block.

Fusing Clover Mini Bias To Tansy & Coneflower Duet

1. For leaves it is easy to begin and end Mini Bias raw edges under the long stems of flowers and fuse around each leaf.

2. Make Mini Bias stem bend when fusing.

3. First fuse Mini Bias across center of Tansy. Next start and end Mini Bias where Tansy bottom meets stem. Cut end ³⁄₁₆-inch longer and tuck for a neat finished point.

4. For five-petal Coneflower follow the suggested numbered sequence for fusing and sewing the Mini Bias in place. Cut a piece of Mini Bias to figure 8 around two opposite petals. With

remaining fifth petal, tuck beginning and ending raw edges under the figure 8 Mini Bias. This is a suggested fusing order. Fuse Mini Bias in whatever order that works for you.

5. For the four-petal Coneflower follow suggested number sequence for applying, fusing and sewing Mini Bias in place.

Sewing Mini Bias To Tansy & Coneflower Duet

1. Sewing around the Coneflowers requires turning curves sharper. Stop sewing and lift the presser foot slightly to continue sewing around curves. Do not try to sew and drag the presser foot against the fabric as this will stretch and buckle the work especially if the backing, batting, and the quilt block are sandwiched together.

**Press pieces in place
and sew in this order:**
1 – Vase
2 – Stems
3 – Leaves
4 – Flowers

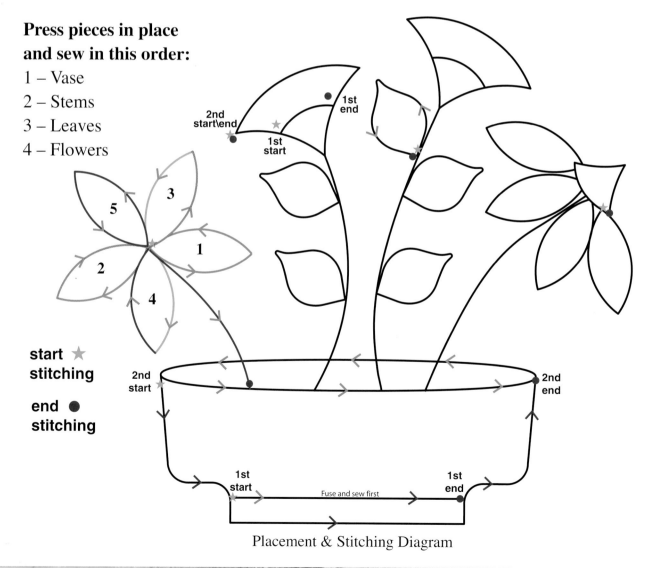

Placement & Stitching Diagram

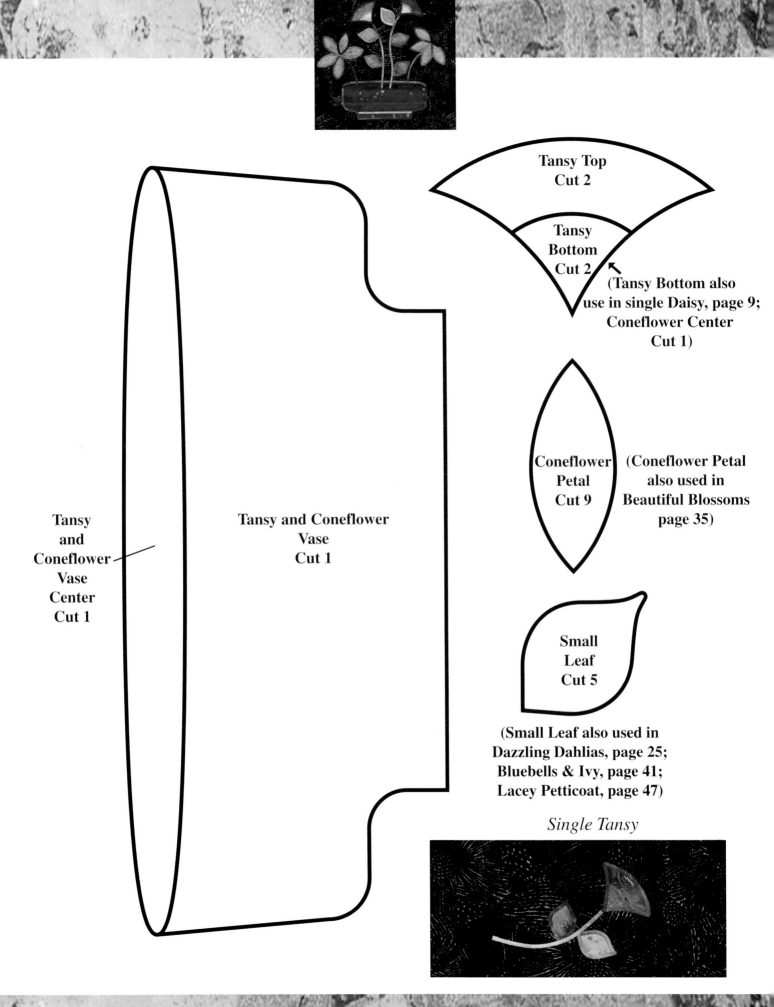

**Tansy Top
Cut 2**

**Tansy
Bottom
Cut 2**

(Tansy Bottom also
use in single Daisy, page 9;
Coneflower Center
Cut 1)

**Tansy
and
Coneflower
Vase
Center
Cut 1**

**Tansy and Coneflower
Vase
Cut 1**

**Coneflower
Petal
Cut 9**

(Coneflower Petal
also used in
Beautiful Blossoms
page 35)

**Small
Leaf
Cut 5**

(Small Leaf also used in
Dazzling Dahlias, page 25;
Bluebells & Ivy, page 41;
Lacey Petticoat, page 47)

Single Tansy

Wallhanging

Beautiful Blossoms

When creating the larger quilt block design, cut 10 large Blossom petals and 10 small Blossom petals to make two flowers. Cut one of Large Leaf Right and one of Large Leaf Left and one of smaller Leaf. The wallhanging design uses five Large Petals and five Small Petals and one small Leaf.

Placement of Beautiful Blossoms

1. Peel paper from the back of all the pieces.

2. Place the bottom raw edge of the Vase 3 inches up from the bottom edge of the 17-inch square background block centered. Next place Vase Center on top of vase.

3. Lightly position large Blossom petals in place first, then stems and leaves making sure there is room for three leaves.

4. Large Blossom petal edges lie two inches from the raw edge of the block.

5. Large petals have two different pointed ends. One point is more tapered and slender. The other end is more plump. Make sure the tapered ends point inward to the Blossom's center. Bring all five Blossom points as close together as possible without overlapping petal edges. A small star of open space is formed at the center.

6. Fuse small petals on top of the inner points of the large petals so petals meet at the Blossom Center. An ⅛ inch of open space is at Blossom Center. Mini Bias will crisscross over this center and cover all raw edges.

Fusing Clover Mini Bias to Beautiful Blossoms

1. Loosen leaves and stems slightly using the Clover Awl so Mini Bias can slide

under these pieces to cover the raw edges of Vase Center. Leaves are good places to start and stop Mini Bias raw edges.

2. Fuse Mini Bias around leaves next. It is so easy to tuck beginning and ending bias under stems.

3. Fuse Mini Bias around large petals first. Begin at any large petal center and figure 8 the Mini Bias around an opposite petal. Cut end at center. Any ends at this center will tuck under this first figure 8 of Bias.

4. Begin Mini Bias for another petal by tucking raw edge under a neighboring petal at the petal's midpoint. Some raw edges can meet at the flower center. But tuck raw edges under the sides of neighboring bias to minimize bulk at the flower center. All raw edges from large petals should be tucked under before starting small petals.

5. Next, apply Mini Bias around small petals. Begin Bias at center tucking end under Bias. Try to tuck ends in other little places away from center so as not to create too much bulk at center. Figure 8 Bias around small petals and tuck ends under bias used for large petals.

Fuse Mini bias around large petals and miter petal tips in this way:

a) Press the Mini Bias up to the point of the petal tip to be mitered.

b) Lay the Mini Bias down flat against background fabric past the petal tip.

c) Use the Clover Awl, the Clover Mini Iron or your fingernail and press down on the Mini Bias $\frac{1}{16}$ inch parallel to and past the raw edge of the petal as shown.

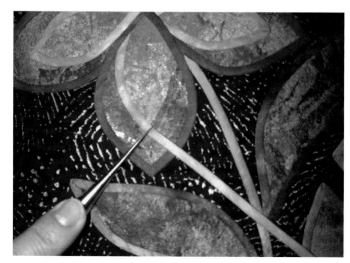

d) While pressing down on the Mini Bias, swing the tail of the Mini Bias over the awl as shown below.

e) A neat mitered pleat at petal tip is formed as shown below.

Sewing Mini Bias to Beautiful Blossoms

1. Sew downward from flower on the stem with small leaf. Then sew continuously around the leaf.

2. Sew downward from flower on other stem.

3. Sew around Vase and Vase Center.

4. Sew around leaves.

5. Sew around larger outer petals.

> NOTE: When sewing through bulky flower center move the wheel of the sewing machine by hand.

6. Sew around inner petals. However, sew as continuously as possible to keep starting and stopping to a minimum. Follow the Bias even if sewing some outer petals and then some inner petals.

Start all petals
from center

Numbers represent
fusing and sewing
sequence for both
large and small petals

start

end

**start ★
stitching**

**end ●
stitching**

Placement Diagram for Quilt

start

end

Placement Diagram for Wallhanging

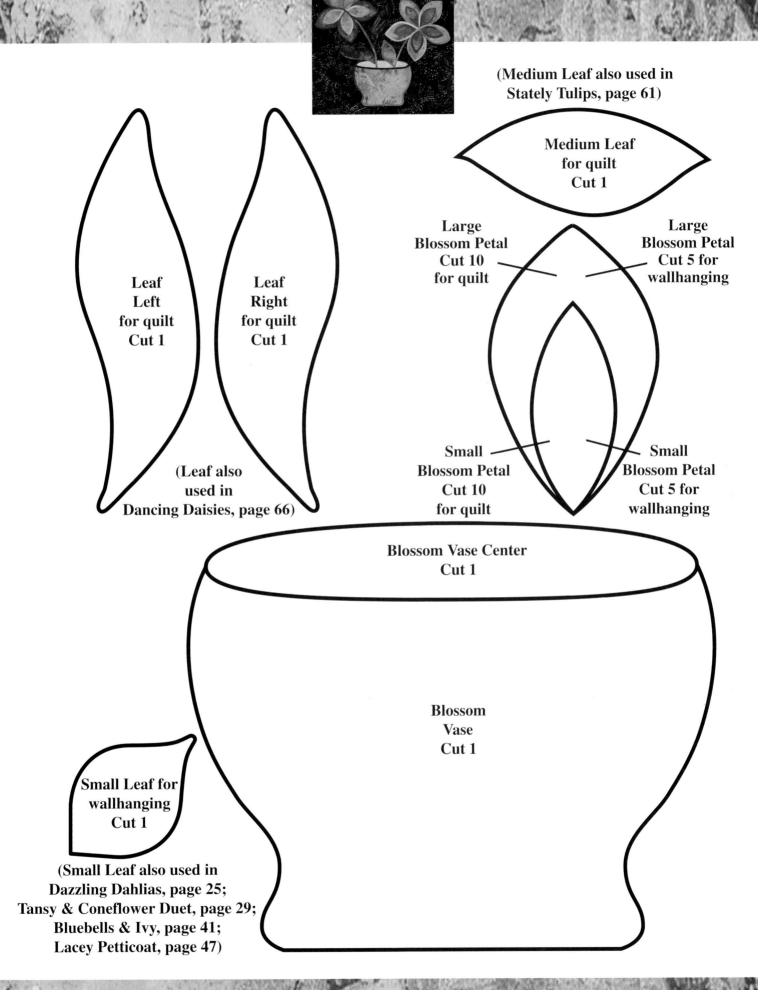

(Medium Leaf also used in
Stately Tulips, page 61)

Medium Leaf
for quilt
Cut 1

Leaf
Left
for quilt
Cut 1

Leaf
Right
for quilt
Cut 1

Large
Blossom Petal
Cut 10
for quilt

Large
Blossom Petal
Cut 5 for
wallhanging

(Leaf also
used in
Dancing Daisies, page 66)

Small
Blossom Petal
Cut 10
for quilt

Small
Blossom Petal
Cut 5 for
wallhanging

Blossom Vase Center
Cut 1

Blossom
Vase
Cut 1

Small Leaf for
wallhanging
Cut 1

(Small Leaf also used in
Dazzling Dahlias, page 25;
Tansy & Coneflower Duet, page 29;
Bluebells & Ivy, page 41;
Lacey Petticoat, page 47)

Bluebells & Ivy

When creating the larger quilt block design, use three additional Bluebell pieces and two additional leaf pieces. The wallhanging design uses five Bluebells and six Leaves.

Wallhanging

Fabric and Clover Mini Bias Needed:

Cut one Vase Center from magenta fabric

Cut one Vase from purple fabric

Cut four Stems from Rainbow Clover Mini Bias
for Quilt or cut two Stems from Rainbow
Clover Mini Bias for Wallhanging

Cut five Bluebells from blue fabric for Wallhanging
or cut 8 Bluebells from blue fabric for Quilt

Cut six Leaves from green fabric for Wallhanging
or cut eight Leaves from green fabric for Quilt

Four yards of Clover Rainbow Mini Bias
for Wallhanging or 5¾ yards of Clover
Rainbow Mini Bias for Quilt

**Press pieces in place
and sew in this order:**

1 – Vase

2 – Stems

3 – Flowers

4 – Leaves

Placement of Bluebells & Ivy

1. Peel paper from the back of all the pieces.

2. Place the bottom raw edge of the Vase 3 inches up from the bottom edge of the 17-inch square background block centered. Next place Vase Center on top of vase.

3. Bluebells and leaves alternate on their respective stems to fill the spaces evenly. The tops of Bluebells need to overlap onto stem so that a neat tuck with Clover Mini Bias can be made at the top of the bells.

Fusing Clover Mini Bias to Bluebells & Ivy

1. Begin with a raw edge of the Clover Mini Bias at the top of a Bluebell. Fuse the Mini Bias all around the bell. Make the tail end of the Mini Bias overlap the beginning raw edge. Crease the fold and tuck it under the beginning edge.

2. The bottom curves of each bell can be gracefully made. Allow the Clover Mini Iron to heat the bias and bend while pressing. If a couple of small pleats are taken at these points, worry not because once sewn, the pleats will be concealed. Bending the Mini Bias around the bells takes practice. Sometimes there may be pleats at the corners and sometimes smooth curves. But either way, once sewed down with a twin needle and clear thread, it is nearly impossible to see a difference.

Sewing Bluebells & Ivy

1. Sew the Vase.

2. Sew around a top leaf or bell and then sew straight down the stem. If needed, sew right over the tops of the bells while sewing down the stems.

3. Leaves are fun and easy to sew. Make sure the twin needles take a stitch right into the point of each leaf to hold leaf tips in place securely.

4. Finish sewing the Bluebells. Lift the presser foot slightly while sewing the curves. Do not try to pull the fabric and drag the presser foot against the Clover Mini Bias.

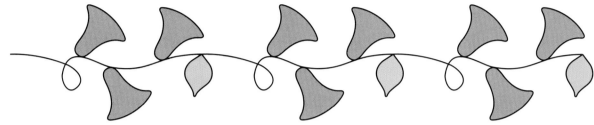

Connect small Bluebell vines
end to end and create a
border design

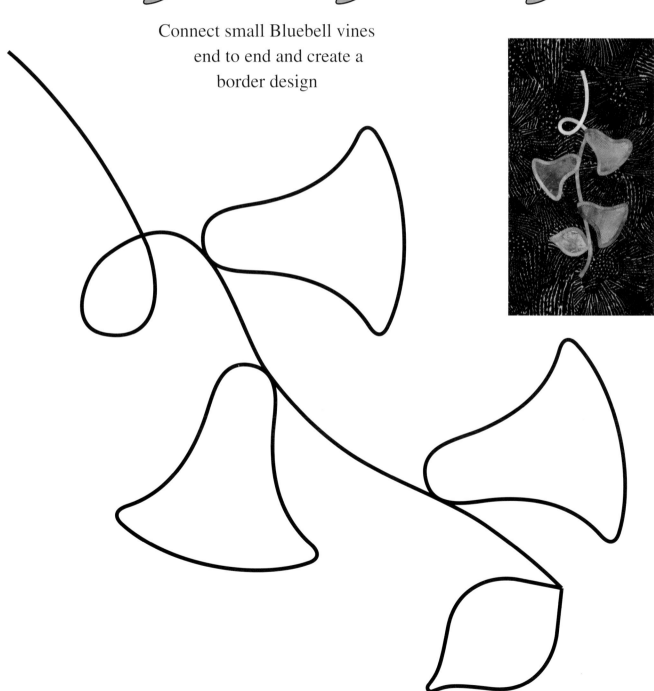

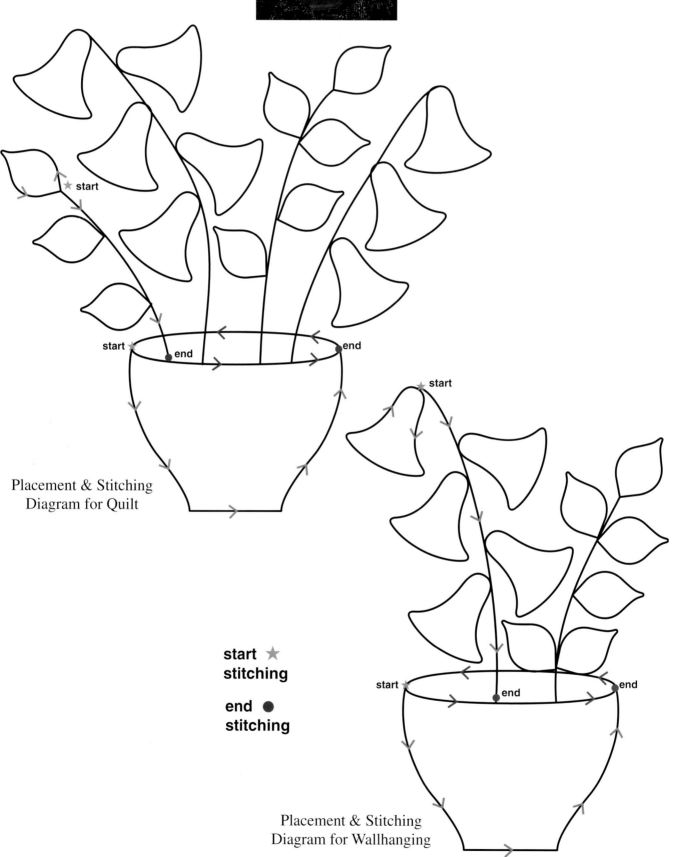

Placement & Stitching
Diagram for Quilt

start ★
stitching

end ●
stitching

Placement & Stitching
Diagram for Wallhanging

Small Leaf also used in
Dazzling Dahlias, page 25;
Tansy & Coneflower Duet, page 29;
Beautiful Blossoms, page 35;
Lacey Petticoats, page 47)

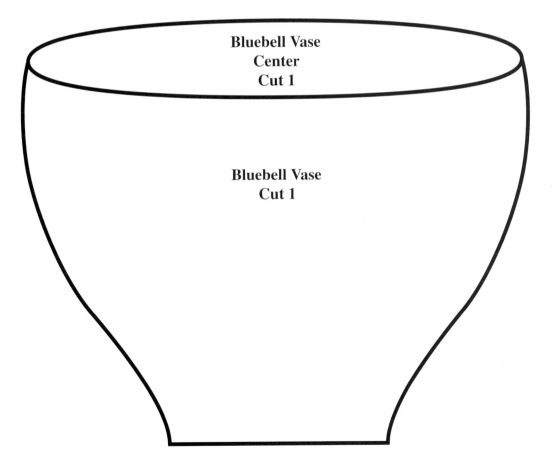

Small Leaf
Cut 8 for quilt
Cut 6 for
wallhanging

Bell
Flower
Cut 8 for quilt
Cut 5 for wallhanging

Bluebell Vase
Center
Cut 1

Bluebell Vase
Cut 1

Lacey Petticoats

When creating the larger quilt block design, add two medium leaves and two small leaves. These leaves can easily be added to the wallhanging as well if desired. The three fabrics chosen for the Lacey Flowers should have very strong color gradation to make these flowers zing.

Wallhanging

Fabric and Clover Mini Bias Needed:

Cut one Vase Center from green fabric

Cut one Vase from purple fabric

Cut three Stems from Rainbow Clover Mini Bias

Cut six Lacey Flowers – two from yellow fabric,
   two from orange fabric and one from red-orange fabric

Cut two Small Leaves from green fabric

Cut two Medium Leaves from green fabric,
   one right, one left

2¾ yards of Clover Rainbow Mini Bias for
   Wallhanging or 3¾ yards of Clover Rainbow
   Mini Bias for Quilt

**Press pieces in place
and sew in this order:**
   1 – Vase
   2 – Stems
   3 – Flowers
   4 – Leaves

Placement of Lacey Petticoats

1. Peel paper from the back of all the pieces.

2. Place the bottom raw edge of the Vase 3 inches up from the bottom edge of the 17-inch square background block centered. Next place Vase Center on top of vase.

3. Use awl to loosen Vase. Tuck raw edges of stems over base center inside Vase.

4. Layer three sets of two Ruffle Flowers together as in photo. Top raw edge of center Ruffle Flower lies three inches down from top raw edge of background block.

5. Remaining two flowers are slightly under and below the bottom tips of the center Ruffle Flower.

6. Place leaves to fill spaces under flowers.

Fusing Clover Mini Bias to Lacey Petticoats

1. With the tip of the awl loosen the stems that lie over Mini Bias that cover the Vase Center.

2. Slide Mini Bias under stems and fuse.

3. On the wallhanging fuse a bias strip across the Vase.

4. On quilt, the purple Vase has variegated purple mini bias, which is fussy cut. To do this, piece one section of purple Mini Bias across the top edge of Vase. Piece a second piece of purple Mini Bias down one side and across the bottom of the Vase. A third piece of purple Mini Bias runs up the last side of the Vase. All raw edges are tucked under.

5. For Lacey Flower, fuse Mini Bias to back Ruffle first. Raw edges will be covered by the front Ruffle.

6. Start fusing bias at the bottom point of the Lacey Flower where stem meets flower. Apply heat to the Mini Bias on the curves and make small pleats at each inward curve. Bias can start and stop at flower outside corner also if necessary.

7. To end, tuck and fold Mini Bias under raw edge of Ruffle bottom edge where bias started.

Sewing Mini Bias to Lacey Petticoats

1. Sew Mini Bias to Vase.

2. Start sewing bias at the bottom point of the Lacey Flower where stem meets flower. Sew around this inside ruffle and then down the stem toward the Vase.

3. Sew bias to the ruffled curves slowly. At each inside curve, lift the presser foot, turn the work and continue sewing. The sewing machine can be set to a slow speed while sewing the Lacey Flower, if available.

4. Sew Bias to outer edge of each Lacey Flower and to leaves.

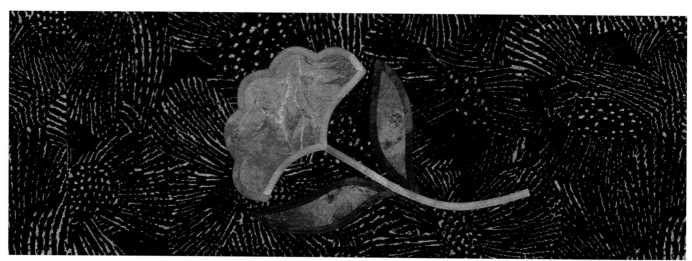

One ruffle from Lacey Petticoat makes this single flower.

Use scallops to make borders of any size.

Border Poppy, page 55.

Border small leaf, page 67.

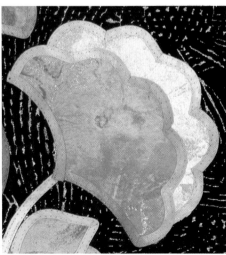

Lacey Petticoat.

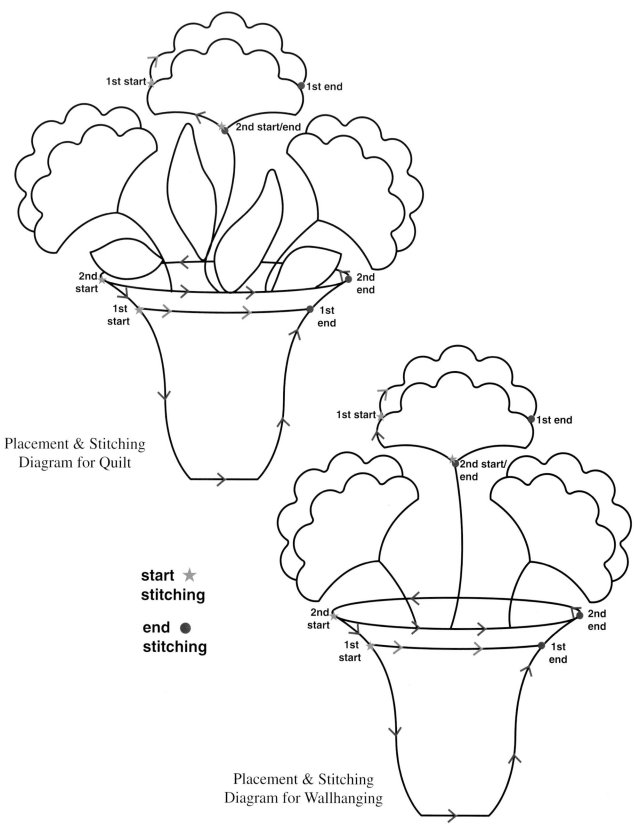

1st start

1st end

2nd start/end

2nd start

2nd end

1st start

1st end

Placement & Stitching
Diagram for Quilt

start ★
stitching

end ●
stitching

1st start

1st end

2nd start/
end

2nd start

2nd end

1st start

1st end

Placement & Stitching
Diagram for Wallhanging

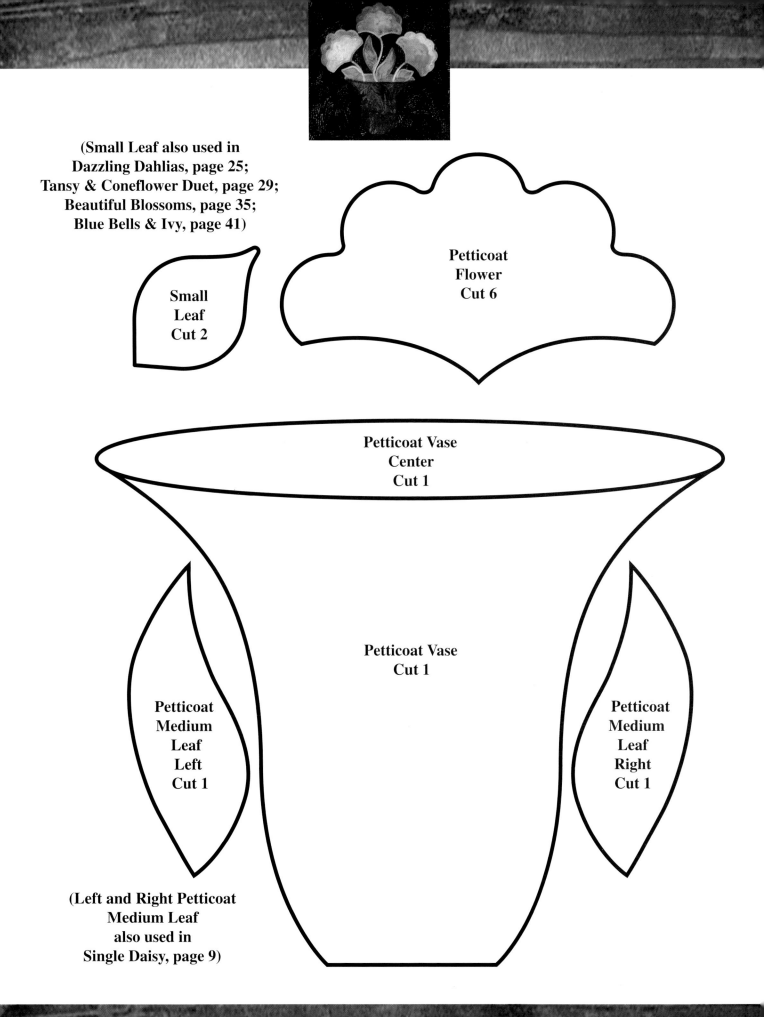

(Small Leaf also used in
Dazzling Dahlias, page 25;
Tansy & Coneflower Duet, page 29;
Beautiful Blossoms, page 35;
Blue Bells & Ivy, page 41)

Small
Leaf
Cut 2

Petticoat
Flower
Cut 6

Petticoat Vase
Center
Cut 1

Petticoat Vase
Cut 1

Petticoat
Medium
Leaf
Left
Cut 1

Petticoat
Medium
Leaf
Right
Cut 1

(Left and Right Petticoat
Medium Leaf
also used in
Single Daisy, page 9)

Wallhanging

Waltzing Irises

When creating the larger quilt block design, use six additional leaf pieces. The wallhanging design does not use leaves, but leaves can be added.

Fabric and Clover Mini Bias Needed:

Cut one Vase Center from green fabric

Cut one Vase from blue to green fabric

Cut three green Stems from Rainbow Clover Mini Bias

Cut three Iris Leaf Right from green fabric for quilt block

Cut three Iris Leaf Left from yellow to green fabric for quilt block

Cut eight Iris Petal Right from lavender shades of fabric for quilt or wallhanging

Cut seven Iris Petal Left from lavender shades of fabric for quilt or wallhanging

4½ yards of Rainbow Clover Mini Bias for the wallhanging and 6¼ yards for the quilt

1. Peel paper from the back of all the pieces.

2. Place the bottom raw edge of the Vase 3 inches up from the bottom edge of the 17-inch square background block centered. Next place Vase Center on top of vase.

3. Middle Iris petal top lies three inches from block raw edge. Place an Iris on each side of the center flower.

4. Stems begin ½" under Iris Center and end in Vase.

5. Six leaves – three right and three left – are tucked inside vase at different heights. These leaves bend to fit between the spaces among the stems.

Sewing Mini Bias on Waltzing Irises

1. For five-petal Iris flower follow the suggested numbered sequence on the placement diagram for fusing and sewing the Mini Bias in place. Cut a piece of Mini Bias to figure 8 around two opposite petals. Then with remaining fifth petal, tuck beginning and ending raw edges under the figure 8 Mini Bias. This is a suggested fusing sequence.

NOTE: Once familiar with this sewing path, you can change the sewing path as needed depending on the direction sewn. If preferred sew iris petals down in your own way.

COLOR CLUE: Let the colors of the Rainbow Mini Bias flow and show! Every bias stem to a flower does not have to be 100 percent green. Look at the stems on the Waltzing Iris block. Orange blends into yellow green near leaves. That little bit of orange makes the colors really pop!

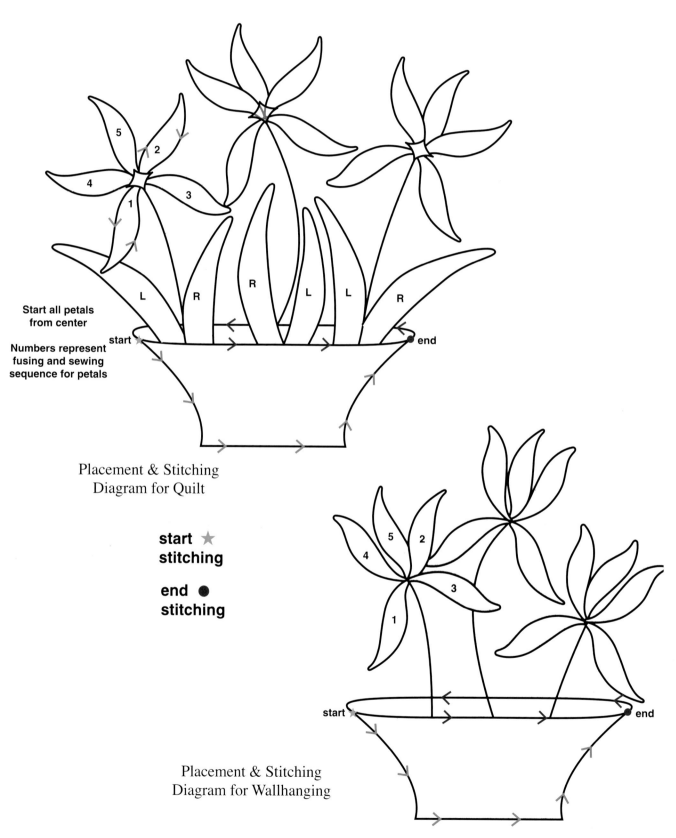

Start all petals from center

Numbers represent fusing and sewing sequence for petals

start

end

Placement & Stitching
Diagram for Quilt

start ★
stitching

end ●
stitching

start

end

Placement & Stitching
Diagram for Wallhanging

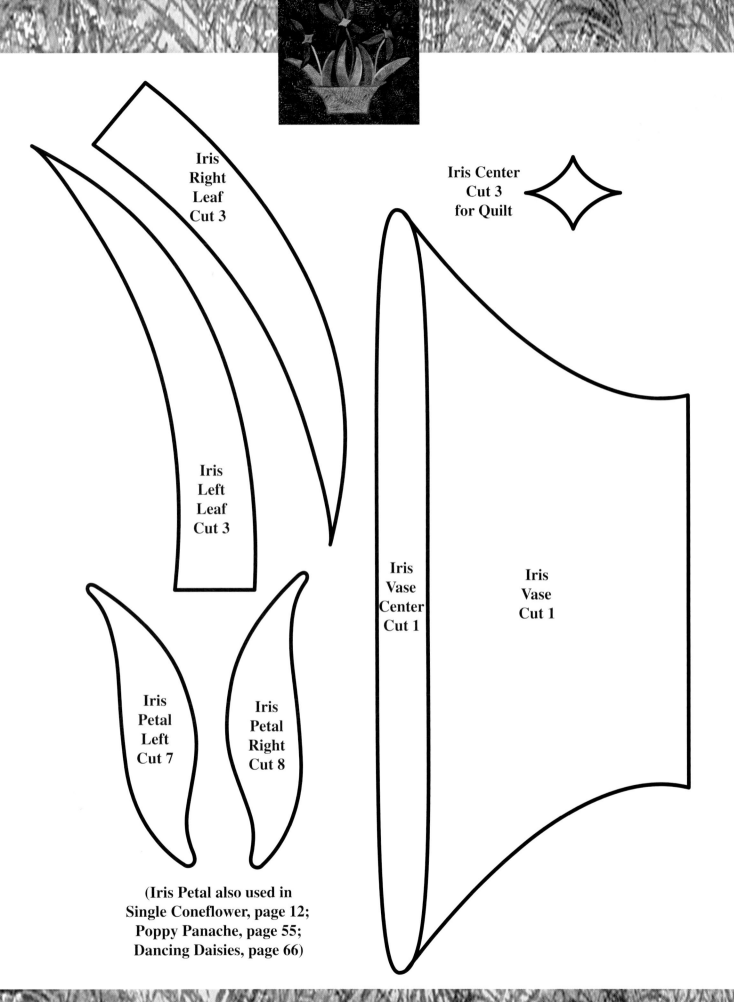

Iris
Right
Leaf
Cut 3

Iris Center
Cut 3
for Quilt

Iris
Left
Leaf
Cut 3

Iris
Vase
Center
Cut 1

Iris
Vase
Cut 1

Iris
Petal
Left
Cut 7

Iris
Petal
Right
Cut 8

(Iris Petal also used in
Single Coneflower, page 12;
Poppy Panache, page 55;
Dancing Daisies, page 66)

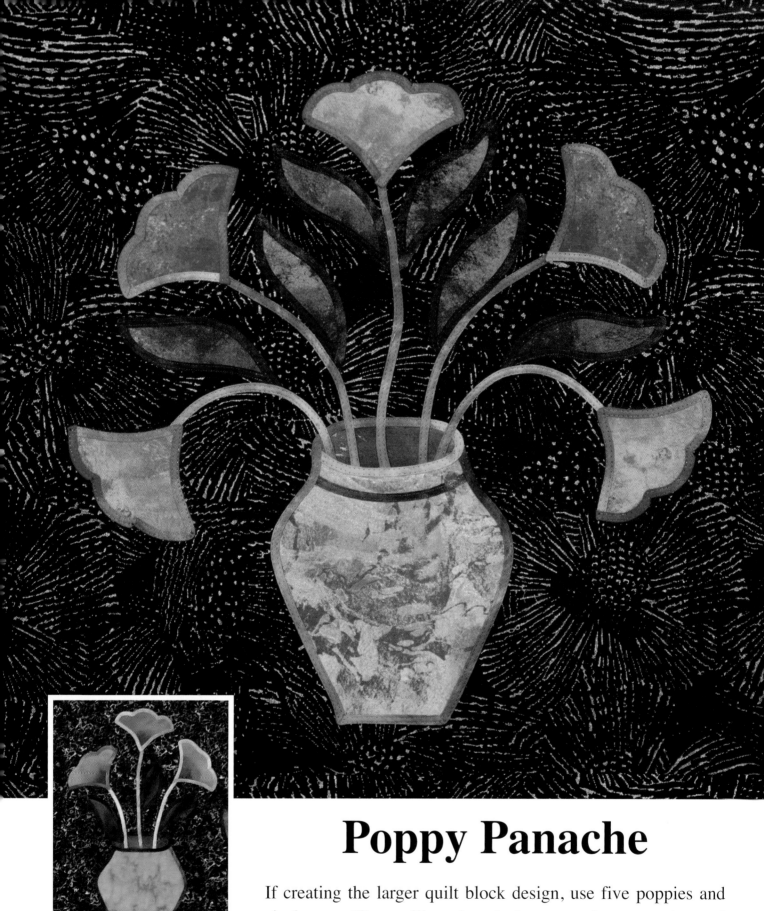

Wallhanging

Poppy Panache

If creating the larger quilt block design, use five poppies and six leaves. The wallhanging design uses three poppies and three leaves.

Fabric and Clover Mini Bias Needed:

Cut one Vase Center from magenta fabric

Cut one Vase from green fabric

Cut three Stems from Rainbow Clover Mini Bias for Wallhanging or

    Cut five Stems from Rainbow Clover Mini Bias for Quilt

Cut three Poppies from orange fabric for Wallhanging or

    Cut five Poppies from orange fabric for Quilt

Cut three Leaves from purple fabric for Wallhanging or

    Cut six Leaves from purple fabric for Quilt

2½ yards of Rainbow Clover Mini Bias for Wallhanging or

3¾ yard of Rainbow Clover Mini Bias for Quilt

Placement of Poppy Panache

1. Peel paper from the back of all the pieces.

2. Place the bottom raw edge of the Vase 3 inches up from the bottom edge of the 17-inch square background block centered. Next place Vase Center on top of vase.

3. Place the center Poppy three inches down from the top raw edge of the 17-inch square background block.

4. Place the two lower Poppies three inches in from the raw edges of the 17-inch square background block.

5. Place the two remaining Poppies between the three already in position and place leaves as shown in photographs.

Fusing Clover Mini Bias to Poppy Panache

1. The stems of the Poppies nearest the Vase show just how much Clover Mini Bias can curve so put plenty of bend in these two stems.

2. Start and end Clover Mini Bias for each leaf under flower stems.

Sewing Bias to Poppy Panache

1. Start fusing Mini Bias at one corner of the Poppy but not at the corner by the stem. To create full curves on Poppies, make a full pleat in Mini Bias between scallops.

2. To end fusing Mini Bias around Poppy, cut end ³⁄₁₆-inch longer and tuck under beginning of Mini Bias for a neat finished point.

Leaves can be rotated and used in any position

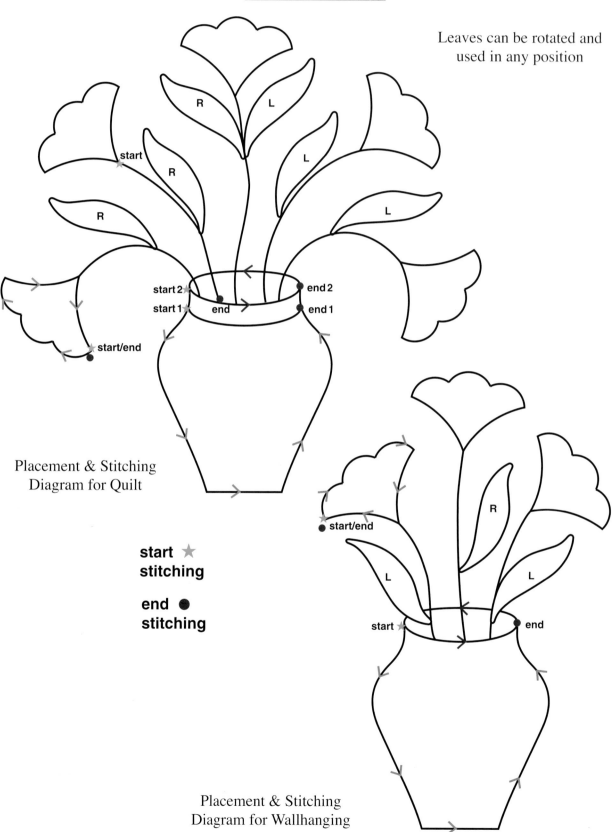

start

R　　　L

R

R　　　L

L

start 2 ★　　　● end 2

start 1 ★　end →　end 1

★ start/end
●

Placement & Stitching Diagram for Quilt

start ★
stitching

end ●
stitching

● start/end

R

L　　　L

start ★　　　● end

Placement & Stitching Diagram for Wallhanging

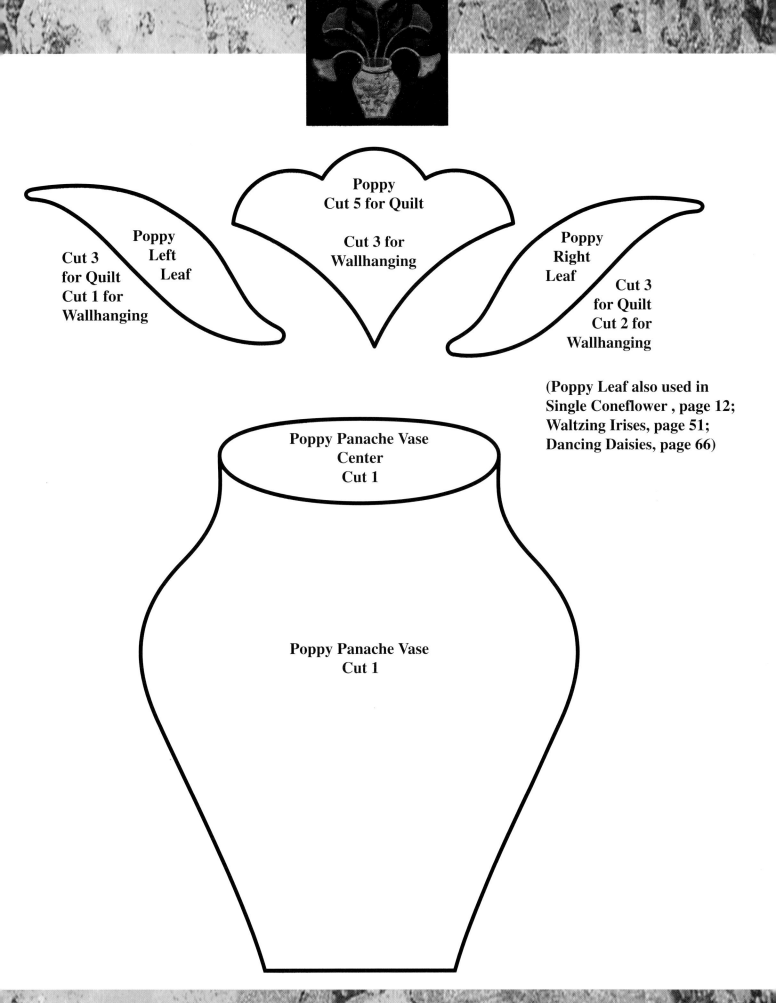

Poppy
Cut 5 for Quilt

Cut 3 for
Wallhanging

Poppy
Left
Leaf

Cut 3
for Quilt
Cut 1 for
Wallhanging

Poppy
Right
Leaf

Cut 3
for Quilt
Cut 2 for
Wallhanging

(Poppy Leaf also used in
Single Coneflower , page 12;
Waltzing Irises, page 51;
Dancing Daisies, page 66)

Poppy Panache Vase
Center
Cut 1

Poppy Panache Vase
Cut 1

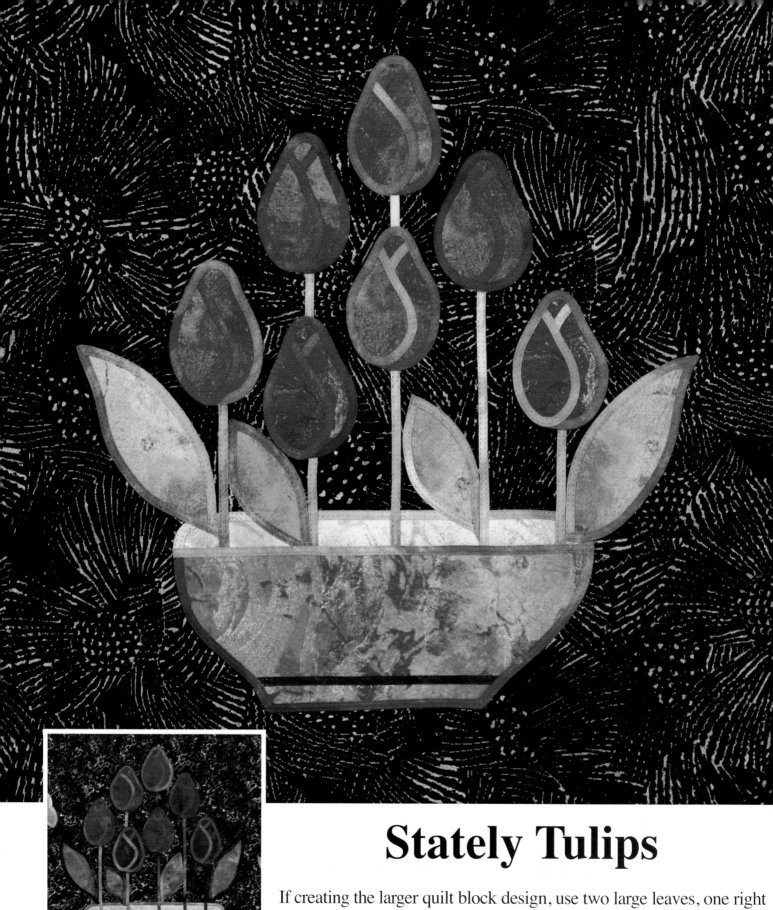

Stately Tulips

If creating the larger quilt block design, use two large leaves, one right and one left and two medium left leaves. The wallhanging design uses two large leaves, one right and one left, one medium right leaf, and one small leaf. The Tulips are the same for both blocks.

Wallhanging block

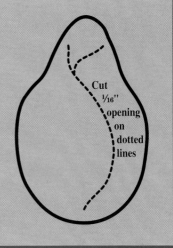

Fabric and Clover Mini Bias Needed:

Cut one Vase Center from yellow fabric

Cut one Vase from orange fabric

Cut five blue and purple Stems from Clover Rainbow Mini Bias

Cut two large Leaves, one right and one left from green fabric

Cut one medium Leaf from green fabric

Cut one small Leaf from green fabric

Cut seven Tulips from magenta fabric

Five yards Clover Rainbow Mini Bias

Cut
1/16"
opening
on
dotted
lines

1. *Make a **plastic template** for tulip: Draw inner lines of tulip on template plastic. Cut a 1/16-inch opening on the inner pencil lines starting 1/8-inch in from template outer edge.*

2. *Lay template on top of right side of tulip fabric piece and draw a pencil line in the channel to mark the Mini Bias placement lines onto the right side of all tulip pieces.*

Placement of Stately Tulips

1. Peel paper from the back of all the pieces.

2. Place the bottom raw edge of the Vase 3 inches up from the bottom edge of the 17-inch square background block centered. Next place Vase Center on top of vase.

3. The top edge of the top center Tulip lies exactly centered horizontally and 2½ inches down from raw edge of 17-inch square background block.

4. Place another Tulip directly below this top center Tulip. Bottom raw edge of top Tulip lies ¾ inch above the top edge of the Tulip below it. This placement is necessary so one strip of Clover Mini Bias can run straight down through these two Tulips.

5. Place another Tulip to the left of the center Tulip and slightly below so that it and yet a third Tulip are descending in height. See placement diagram.

6. Place another Tulip below the Tulip that is just to the left of the center tulip. This Tulip lies directly below this second Tulip so one strip of Clover Mini Bias can run straight down through these two Tulips. See placement diagram.

7. Repeat placement of two more Tulips descending in height to the right of the center Tulip. See placement diagram.

8. Place Clover Mini Bias under Tulips and straight downward into basket.

9. Place leaves according to diagram last.

10. When confident of placement, lightly press pieces in place. Edges of some pieces may need to be loosened here and there for placement of Clover Mini Bias. Use the Clover Awl to loosen Mini Bias that has been ironed in place and to slide the edge of Mini Bias for vase under stems.

Fusing Clover Mini Bias To Stately Tulips

1. Slide scissor tip or awl under Tulip bottoms to loosen fusing so a ¼ inch of Clover Mini Bias can slide up under Tulip piece. Repeat this procedure to loosen fusing in vase top edge so Clover Mini Bias can slide under ¼ inch also.

2. When fusing Mini Bias to Tulips, make Mini Bias curve as much as possible to emphasize the curves of this flower. The curves on one Tulip may be more dramatic than another. Variation in the look of the curves is fine.

3. Making Color Zing on Tulips: Fussy cut Mini Bias so just little bits of yellow, mostly orange and mostly red surround magenta-colored fabric Tulips. Vary colors around each tulip as shown in color photos of the Stately Tulips Block. Orange and red Mini Bias next to magenta fabric make all these colors pop.

Sewing Stately Tulips

1. Twin needle stitch stems first starting at the top of the stem nearest the Tulip and sewing downward to Vase. Sewing stems first stabilizes the whole piece.

2. Next, twin needle stitch around Vase. On upper edge of Vase, either back tack at each little section of the Vase edge on one model, or stitch right over the stems. It is your choice.

3. Next, twin needle stitch leaves starting and stopping mini bias neatly under stems.

4. Lastly, twin needle stitch Tulips. Start at the right hand edge of the short piece. Sew into the middle of the Tulip. Then stitch backward up center line and stitch down and around entire Tulip.

Place Tulips together to form another block or border.

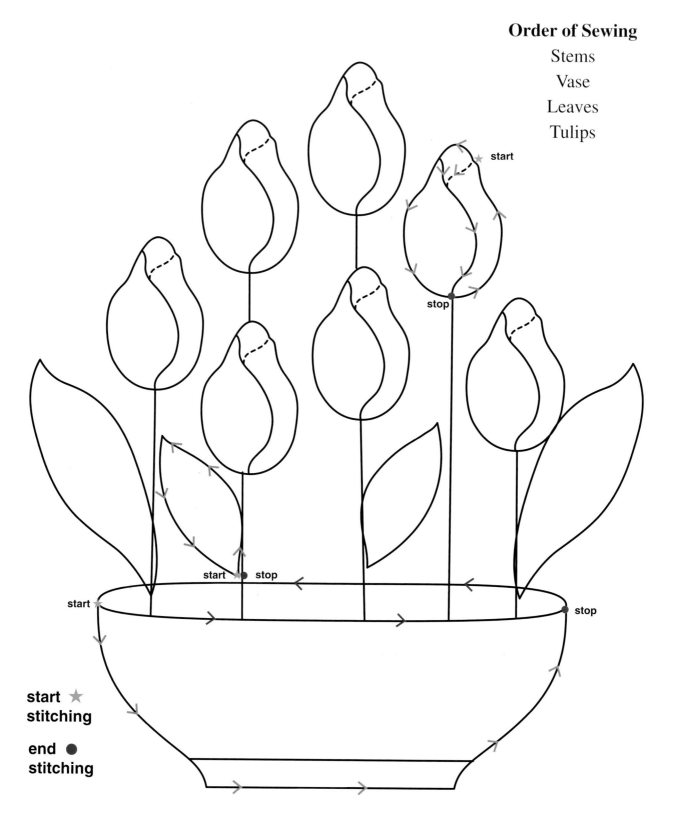

Order of Sewing
Stems
Vase
Leaves
Tulips

start

stop

start ⭐ stop

start

stop

start ⭐
stitching

end ●
stitching

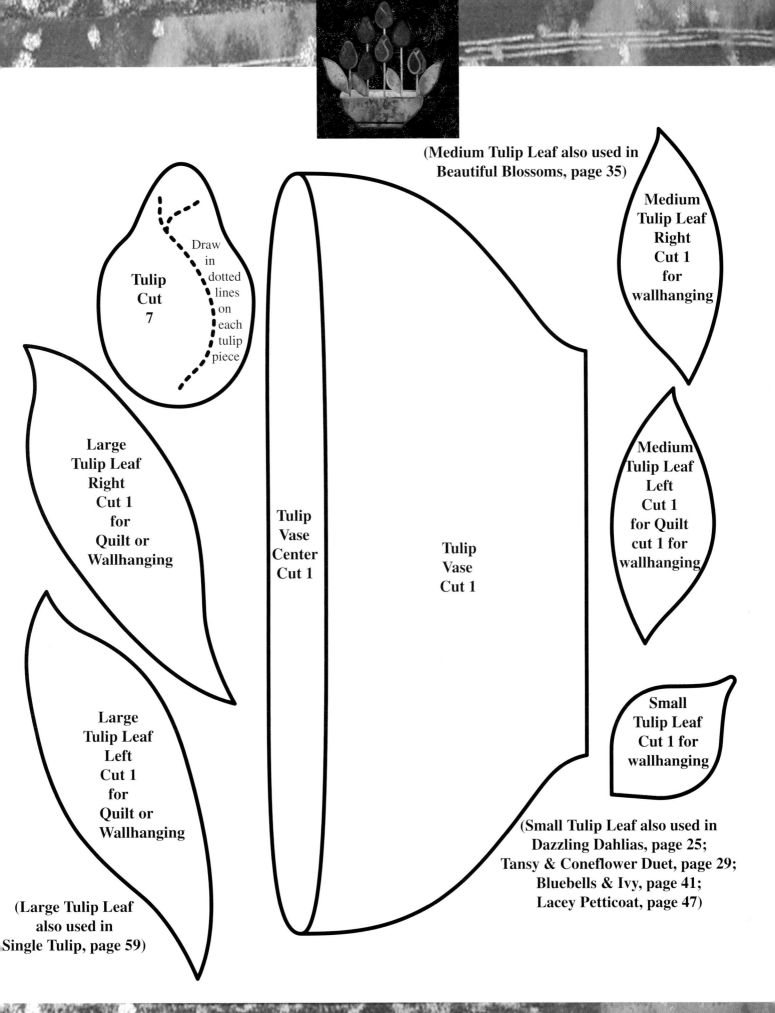

(Medium Tulip Leaf also used in
Beautiful Blossoms, page 35)

Medium
Tulip Leaf
Right
Cut 1
for
wallhanging

Draw
in
dotted
lines
on
each
tulip
piece

Tulip
Cut
7

Medium
Tulip Leaf
Left
Cut 1
for Quilt
cut 1 for
wallhanging

Large
Tulip Leaf
Right
Cut 1
for
Quilt or
Wallhanging

Tulip
Vase
Center
Cut 1

Tulip
Vase
Cut 1

Large
Tulip Leaf
Left
Cut 1
for
Quilt or
Wallhanging

Small
Tulip Leaf
Cut 1 for
wallhanging

(Large Tulip Leaf
also used in
Single Tulip, page 59)

(Small Tulip Leaf also used in
Dazzling Dahlias, page 25;
Tansy & Coneflower Duet, page 29;
Bluebells & Ivy, page 41;
Lacey Petticoat, page 47)

Wallhanging block

Dancing Daisies

When creating the larger quilt block design, cut 24 petals and three Daisy centers and two medium leaves. For the wallhanging design cut eight petals, and one daisy center and two large leaves. Photo at left shows nine petals, but the flower is easiest to make with eight petals.

Fabric and Clover Mini Bias Needed:

Cut one Vase Center piece from tangerine fabric

Cut one Vase piece from fuchsia fabric

Cut one Stem from Rainbow Clover Mini Bias for Wallhanging or

Cut three Stems from Rainbow Clover Mini Bias for Quilt

Cut two large Leaves, a right and a left piece from green
fabric for Wallhanging

Cut two medium Leaves for Quilt

Cut eight Daisy Petals from yellow fabric for Wallhanging or cut 24 Daisy Petals,
eight from yellow fabric, eight from orange and eight from pink fabric for Quilt

Cut one Daisy Center from purple fabric for Wallhanging

Cut three Daisy Centers from purple fabric for Quilt

Three yards of Clover Rainbow Mini Bias for Wallhanging or

6½ yards of Clover Rainbow Mini Bias for Quilt

**NOTE:** If placing yellow fabric on a dark background fabric, cut two of each yellow petal to line the petal so the dark fabric will not shadow through petals.

Placement of Dancing Daisies

1. Peel paper from the back of all the pieces.

2. Place the bottom raw edge of the Vase 3 inches up from the bottom edge of the 17-inch square background block centered. Next place Vase Center on top of vase.

3 Pointed ends of petals meet at the center of the daisy with a ½ inch of space left at center.

4. Place a petal at each of the compass points first – north, south, east and west.

5. Next, place petals in between each of these petals.

6. Press petals in place.

Fusing Clover Mini Bias to Dancing Daisies

1. Start and end raw edges of Mini Bias at any petal center.

2. Press bias around petal. On curve apply the heat of the Mini Iron while continuously curving the bias. A tiny pleat

may be taken on this curve, if desired. This pleat will not show once bias is sewed in place with a twin needle.

3. Press Daisy Center in place making sure all mini bias is tucked under center.

4. Press mini bias around center leaving an extra ⅜ inch.

5. Tuck this extra end under the beginning Mini Bias that has already been pressed in place. To do this, peel up beginning Mini Bias, tuck tail under and press again.

Sewing Dancing Daisies

1. Sew bias stems in place.

2. Sew Vase.

3. Begin sewing Mini Bias continuously at the center of any petal. Lift presser foot while sewing curves. Do not pull fabric on curves. Sew around petal ending with needle up.

5. Pivot block so that the twin needle is lined up at the center point of the neighboring petal. Sew around this petal and continue until all petals are sewn.

6. Sew Daisy Center last. Make sure to take a couple of stitches and then lift the presser foot to realign the needles on the bias all the way around the flower center.

Order of Sewing
Stems
Vase
Leaves
Daisy
Daisy Center

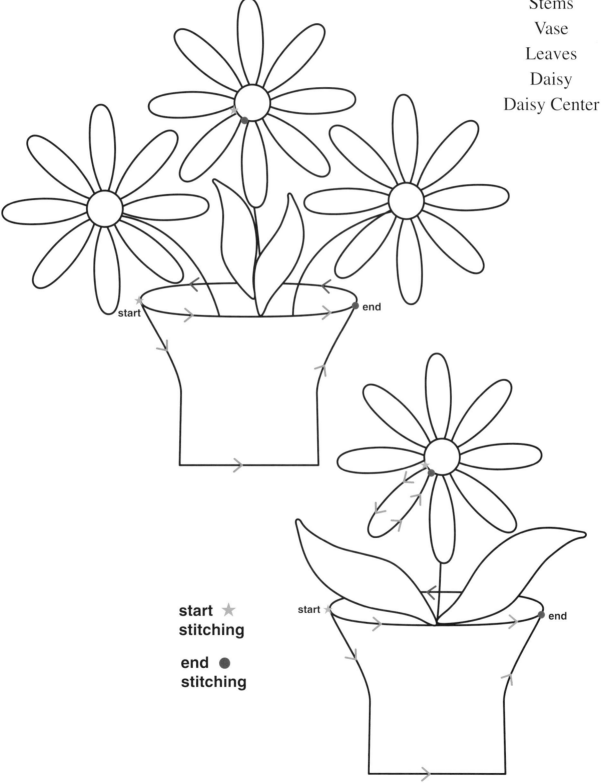

start

end

start ⭐
stitching

end ●
stitching

start

start

end

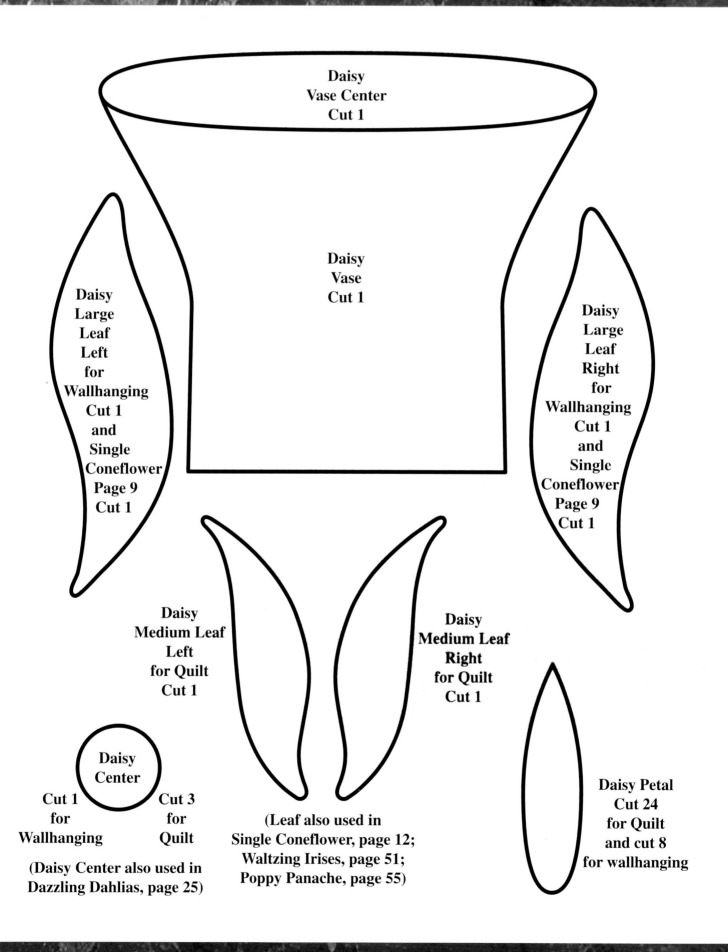

Daisy
Vase Center
Cut 1

Daisy
Vase
Cut 1

Daisy
Large
Leaf
Left
for
Wallhanging
Cut 1
and
Single
Coneflower
Page 9
Cut 1

Daisy
Large
Leaf
Right
for
Wallhanging
Cut 1
and
Single
Coneflower
Page 9
Cut 1

Daisy
Medium Leaf
Left
for Quilt
Cut 1

Daisy
Medium Leaf
Right
for Quilt
Cut 1

Daisy
Center

Cut 1
for
Wallhanging

Cut 3
for
Quilt

(Daisy Center also used in
Dazzling Dahlias, page 25)

(Leaf also used in
Single Coneflower, page 12;
Waltzing Irises, page 51;
Poppy Panache, page 55)

Daisy Petal
Cut 24
for Quilt
and cut 8
for wallhanging

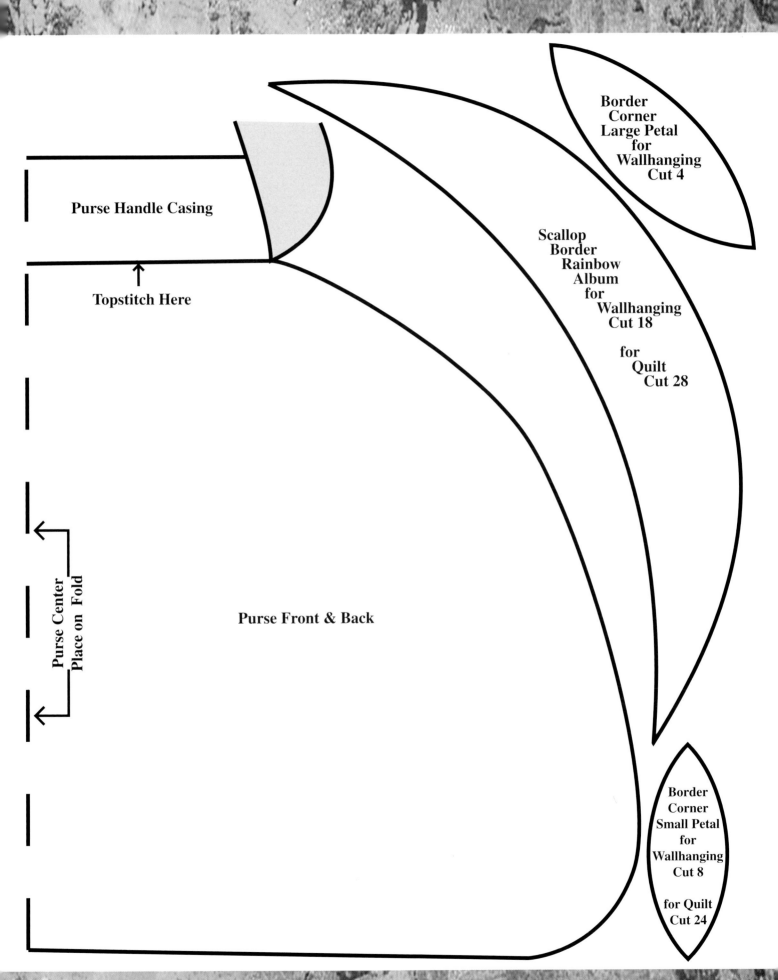

Purse Handle Casing

Topstitch Here

Border
Corner
Large Petal
for
Wallhanging
Cut 4

Scallop
Border
Rainbow
Album
for
Wallhanging
Cut 18

for
Quilt
Cut 28

Purse Center
Place on Fold

Purse Front & Back

Border
Corner
Small Petal
for
Wallhanging
Cut 8

for Quilt
Cut 24

Putting Your Quilt Together

1. Square up each of the nine blocks to 16½" and each of the six half blocks to 8½" x 16½" for the quilt.

2. Machine piece each block together by sewing the seam allowances of the quilt blocks together. Push the batting and backing aside to sew this seam.

3. Press each seam open.

4. At quilt back, trim away excess batting so batting meets neatly at seam.

5. Fold under backing fabric a ¼-inch. Clover 5mm Fusible Web Tape can be ironed in place on one side of the block. Lay the folded edge of the neighboring block on top of the fusible web and iron this seam in place.

6. Following suggested quilt block layout, begin to sew each block together creating three vertical rows of blocks.

7. Next, piece the three vertical rows together to form the top.

8. Add borders. For the wallhanging, borders are six inches wide and for the quilt, the borders are eight inches wide.

9. Scallop pattern pieces fit easily around the wallhanging or the quilt. The scallops hug the seam line between the quilt blocks and the border. Since actual fabric measurements of the finished blocks can vary, the scallops can easily fit borders that may vary a bit, too. Scallops measure eight inches wide. These scallops can be placed so that each scallop is touching its neighbor. Or the scallops can be moved from ¼ inch to ½ inch apart to help fill up any extra border space that might be present. Scallop pattern is shown on page 67.

10. For wallhanging, cut 18 scallops. For quilt, cut 28 scallops. Back scallops with Steam-A-Seam 2 Lite and fuse in place. Since the wallhanging fabric was black, Clover black Mini Bias was used to outline applique the scallops. The scallops look like they are floating on the black border fabric by matching the outline bias to the backing fabric.

11. The corner borders for the wallhanging are simply one large almond-shaped leaf and two smaller leaves (pg. 67) placed on either side of the larger leaf. Rainbow Mini Bias outlines these corner pieces so they stand out. The corner borders for the quilt are one Poppy. Use any flower or shape you like at the corners as well.

12. Bind quilt with Clover ¾-inch Rainbow Border Bias for a perfect color match or a binding of choice.

Quilt Block Layout

Dazzling Dahlias	Single Coneflower	Lacey Petticoats
	Beautiful Blossoms	
Single Daisy		Single Bluebell Stalk
Tansy & Coneflower Duet	Dancing Daisies	Bluebells & Ivy
Single Petticoat	Waltzing Irises	Single Tulip
Stately Tulips		Poppy Panache
	Single Tansy	

Other Projects

Easy Gathered Bias Purse

The Gathered Bias Purse can be made very quickly with Clover's gathered bias strip combined with Clover Quick or Miniature Bias. This purse may be made in any size. The gathered bias can be sewn in any direction or any combination of directions. Gathered bias can also be sewn to both the front and back panels of the purse. Here are the complete directions for using gathered bias on the purse front and for making a braided bias handle to match.

Fabric and Clover Gathered Bias Needed:

Small Purse

- 8" x 5" crinoline
- 50" of Clover gathered bias from one Clover Flower Chenille Brooch Kit
- Two 8" x 5" pieces of fabric
- 8" x 5" thin batting
- 7⅓ yards of variegated Clover Quick Bias (Purple, Teal, Blue)

Large Purse

- 8" x 10" crinoline
- Three yards of gathered bias (two Brooch kits).
- Two 8" x 10" pieces of fabric
- 8" x 10" thin batting
- Nine yards of Clover Quick Bias (Earth Tones Brown)

1. Cut crinoline either 8" x 5" or 8" x 10" for size purse preferred.

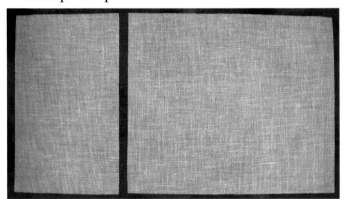

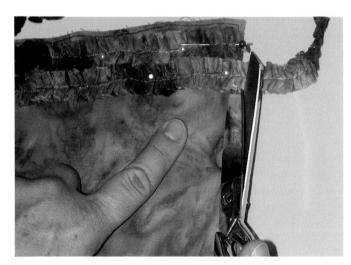

2. Cut fabric in a color to match Clover's gathered bias exact size of crinoline. Lay fabric right side up on top of crinoline. Stay stitch (sew ⅛-inch in from raw edge) on all four sides sewing through crinoline and fabric.

3. Pin rows of gathered bias in place across this purse front allowing ¼-inch seam allowance at top and bottom only. At sides bring gathered bias right to edges and trim as shown.

4. With a single needle in the sewing machine, sew right down the center stitching that holds the gathered bias together. Use an awl and when necessary lift the presser foot and straighten the ruffles under the presser foot before continuing to stitch.

5. Press and fuse ¼-inch Clover Quick Bias or ⅛"-inch Clover Mini Bias centered over center gathering line of stitching. Fuse carefully so Clover Bias lies in neat, straight lines. Ruffles of the gathered bias may flatten with pressing but will fluff up with continued handling.

6. With clear monofilament thread, machine sew with a twin needle over Clover Bias.

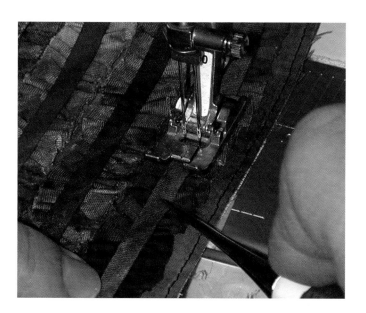

The Braided Bias Purse Handle

Four strips of Clover Quick Bias come together to form one twisted braid handle. The handle at the left and right side of the purse separates and straddles the purse front and back. Beads embellish the handle and mark where the braids end and hide the stitching.

7. Cut four pieces of Clover Quick Bias making sure each piece measures exactly 1½ yards.

8. Place two of these pieces with fusing sides together. Iron neatly. Repeat for other two pieces to form two separate strips.

9. Place the two fused pieces of Clover Quick Bias together so ends line up, and make a chalk mark 7 inches for small purse or 12 inches for larger purse up from the cut ends on one side.

10. Machine sew with a matching color thread or monofilament thread across the chalk mark back tacking to hold these two strips together.

11. Pin the end of the strip nearest the back tacking to a piece of corrugated cardboard to hold all four strips securely for braiding as shown below.

12. Braid these two strips together continuously left over right keeping the strips facing upward. Do not twist the strips. While moving the strip on the left over the strip on the right, allow this left strip to puff up into a cone-shape twist. This helps keep the twist even.

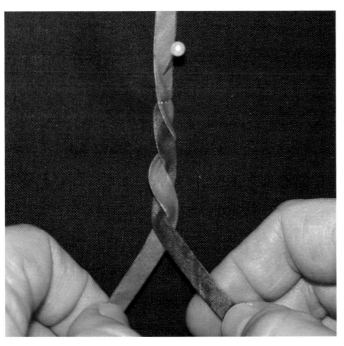

Occasionally tighten up the braid and work at keeping the twists of the braid equal.

13. Stop braiding at 7 inches for small purse or 12 inches for larger purse from raw edge. Pin and make a chalk mark at this point. Look braid over to make sure the twist is even. Back tack at the chalk mark.

Slide Beads on Handle Before Attaching Handle To Purse

14. Slide a bead with a ³⁄₁₆-inch opening up over raw edges so one bead or more will lie right over machine stitching. (Hand or machine embroidery can cover this machine tacking and embellish the purse handle if preferred.) Embroidery can be applied after the handle is attached as well.

15. Place a drop of E6000 fabric glue on stitching and then slide bead over stitching so bead is permanently bonded over stitching. Repeat for other end.

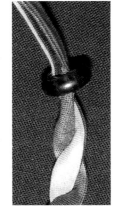

Finishing Gathered Bias Purse
16. Piece back of purse with batting behind. This purse back can be solid fabric or it can also be covered with gathered bias like the purse front.

17. Lay two ends of bias across front of purse and the other two across back of purse. Pin in place. Trap cut bias ends in seam before sewing purse together.

18. Sew bias to purse front and back. Either sew all bias with an invisible applique stitch by hand across purse front and back or machine sew the bias on purse front with a twin needle and then sew the bias on purse back on by hand with an invisible applique stitch. Line purse.

Attaching Purse Clasp

Before sewing lining in place, attach a Clover magnetic purse clasp inside purse.

19. With the Clover Awl make two small holes where purse clasp prongs will go.

20. Make a tiny $\frac{1}{16}$-inch snip with scissors in each hole.

21. Push prongs through holes to back, slide washer over prongs and push prongs outward and flat against clasp. Repeat for other side of clasp.

22. Hand sew purse lining in place.

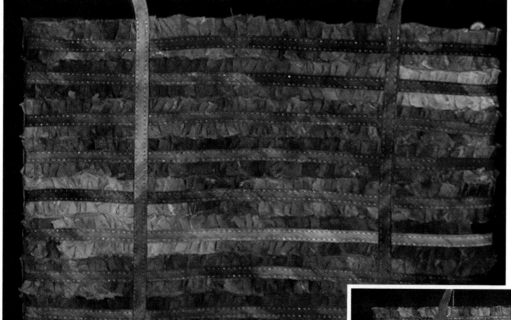

The large purse is made with Earth Tones Brown gathered bias strip. Earth Tones Brown Quick Bias lies over the gathered bias.

The small purse is made of olive gathered bias strip with Purple, Teal, Blue Quick Bias on top.

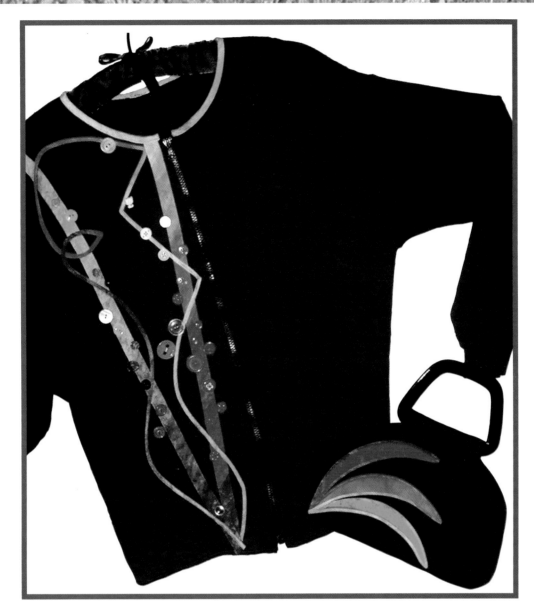

Easy-To-Embellish Purse & Shirt

Materials Needed

Purse

Two yards Rainbow Mini Bias

Three scallop border shapes cut
   from brightly colored fabric

Black purse front and back

Shirt

Black sweatshirt

Three yards Rainbow Border Bias

Two yards Rainbow Quilt Bias or Mini Bias

Jacket zipper

Assorted buttons in colors to match bias

PURSE

The scallop template used to create the border on the Rainbow Album can be used as more than just a border. The Easy-To-Embellish Purse is decorated with this one simple template pattern. Template and pattern on page 67.

1. Cut a purse out using the suggested purse shape or choose a purse shape of your own.

2. Simply fuse three scallops across the purse front making sure that all three pieces share one common point.

3. Rainbow Mini Bias will outline all three scallops and begin and end at his common point. Begin fusing Rainbow Mini Bias at the common point and press the Mini Bias along the top edge of the top scallop. Proceed down the inside edge of this scallop.

4. Continue fusing Mini Bias around remaining scallops. Tuck end under at common point. Finish sewing purse.

SHIRT

1. Cut the shirt open on the center front.

2. Remove knit ribbing from neck edge and shirt bottom by cutting through the ribbing right next to the topstitched edge.

3. Install a black jacket weight zipper at center front of shirt.

4. Start fusing Border Bias at neck edge nearest zipper. Angle the Border Bias straight down the shirt and end the Border Bias two inches to the left of the zipper.

5. The second piece of Border Bias runs from the center of the shoulder seam, down the front of the jacket and meets the first piece of Border Bias.

6. This same piece of Border Bias can continue down the back of the sweatshirt to the bottom back edge of the shirt for a fun embellishment on the back. (This is the only piece of Rainbow Bias that I fused and sewed to the back of the shirt.)

7. Rainbow Quick Bias or Rainbow Mini Bias can be fused in any shape over and around the Border Bias as shown on page 75. Start and end fusing and sewing of Quick Bias or Mini Bias at the bottom edge of the shirt where the Border Bias meets.

8. Sew buttons of all shapes and sizes on top of the Border Bias or Quick Bias matching the colors of the buttons to the Rainbow colors in the bias.

9. Finish neck edge by fusing Border Bias over cut neck edge. Topstitch Border Bias in place around neck edge making sure raw edges are neatly tucked under and stitched down at center front.

Stained Glass Heart Wallhanging using the small Perfect Fit Heart and Clover Rainbow ¼" Quick Bias.

Stained Glass Hearts

Large heart wallhanging 34" x 39"

This wallhanging can be made any size easily because the bias that outlines the fused raw edges of the hearts is applied in continuous lines. The Stained Glass Heart on page 81 shows half hearts on the row ends. These half hearts are optional. The pattern is easier to do leaving the half hearts off.

Other ideas for using these hearts include:

Small heart wallhanging 20½" x 22"

- a single row of hearts can form a quilt border;
- a row of hearts can form a wallhanging;
- a heart on a square makes a potholder;
- a photo in the center heart and names and dates in the surrounding hearts form a memory wallhanging;
- embroidery designs by hand or machine fill hearts for an embellished wallhanging as shown on page 81;

• hearts filled with conversation prints capturing a design inside each heart.

See page 18 for QUICK OVERVIEW OF THE BASIC TECHNIQUE

Refer to the Tools Needed for this technique listed on page 16. Additional materials needed:

- 15 yards of black Clover Quick Bias for large heart wallhanging and 11 yards for small heart wallhanging.
- Two spools of thread color that matches bias in polyester or cotton-covered poly or two spools of YLI Wonder Invisible thread.
- Background fabric: cut 35" x 40" for large heart wallhanging or 21½" x 23" for small heart wallhanging.
- Backing fabric and thin batting each cut ½-inch bigger than background fabric on all sides for either wallhanging.
- ¼ yard of each of five, pre-washed fabrics for hearts in coordinating colors. Hand dyed fabric or batik prints work great.
- 2 yards Lite Steam-A-Seam 2

Prepare Background Fabric

Cut background fabric 35" x 40" for large heart wallhanging. Large heart wallhanging has four rows of hearts and 36 full hearts. Half hearts are optional. Or cut background fabric 21½" x 23" for small wallhanging. Small heart wallhanging has three rows of hearts and 21 full hearts.

NOTE: One row is a line of right-side-up hearts and the upside-down hearts that fit underneath.

2. Make sure background fabric is squared up. (There is an extra inch of background fabric to allow for squaring up when all sewing is completed.)

3. Mark a chalk line three inches down from the top raw edge horizontally across the background fabric and 3 inches in from left side vertically.

Preparing Hearts

4. Make a template of Perfect Fit Heart shape from plastic template material.

5. Carefully trace in pencil either 36 large hearts for large wallhanging or 21 small hearts for small wallhanging onto Lite Steam-A-Seam 2.

HELPFUL HINT – If fabric needs to be fussy cut to fit in hearts an exact way, make a window template with the heart cut out from the center of the plastic so the exact position of the fabric in the heart can be seen.

Cut Out This Heart Center

Plastic

6. Cut hearts out roughly from Lite Steam A-Seam 2 leaving extra paper around pencil lines.

7. Peel paper from one side of Lite Steam A-Seam. Place tacky side face down on wrong side of fabric and press with hot iron for about 6 seconds.

8. Cut each heart out on the pencil line.

Stained Glass Heart Layout

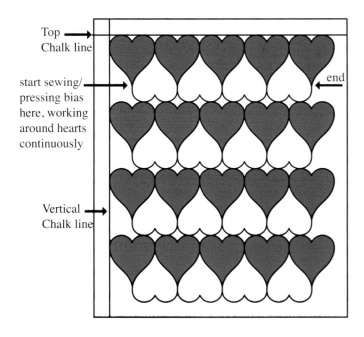

9. Starting with top left heart, lay the first row of hearts on background fabric from left to right. The first heart touches the top horizontal chalk line at its top and touches the left vertical chalk line on its left edge.

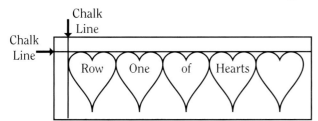

10. Iron first row of hearts in place.

11. Lay the upside-down Perfect Fit Hearts under the first making sure raw edges fit together like a jigsaw puzzle. Hearts can overlap a bit. Press these hearts in place.

12. Repeat for the remaining rows of hearts.

Press Bias To Hearts in Continuous Rows

13. Turn the Clover Mini Iron to "high" and let it warm up on the base about 10 minutes.

14. Starting at the bottom point of the heart at the top left of the wallhanging, press and curve bias around heart shape. Miter with a pleat at heart v-point.

15. Continue fusing Quick Bias in place traveling to upside-down-heart next. Make sure Quick Bias is sticking. If not, leave the iron on the Quick Bias longer.

16. At heart sides, Quick Bias laps exactly on top of the Quick Bias from the neighboring heart. Continue applying Quick Bias until the row is finished.

17. To end this row, cut Quick Bias on a diagonal and tuck raw edge under neighboring heart's bias for a neat finish to the row.

Stained Glass Heart Wallhanging using the small Perfect Fit Heart and Clover Rainbow Purple, Teal, Blue Variagated (¼") Quick Bias.

18. Repeat for the remaining rows.

NOTE: The heart tops in following rows sit on the heart tops from the previous rows. (Occasionally the bias will not lay exactly on top of itself. This is okay and does not affect the look.)

Sew And Quilt In One Step

19. Layer thin batting and backing fabric that is cut one inch larger than background fabric on all sides under the top to form the quilt sandwich and press all layers smoothly.

20. Apply temporary spray adhesive between layers of the wallhanging, smoothing layers with your hands and ironing.

21. Roll wallhanging so that just the top row of hearts to be sewn can be seen.

22. With a twin needle and matching or clear monofilament thread, sew continuously around hearts in first row back tacking at beginning and end of row. Stitch in the exact path the Quick Bias was fused.

NOTE: At heart centers, back tack and then lift the presser foot with the needle up. Plant the presser foot back down and start sewing in the next direction.

23. Press the wallhanging. Do not fear that the hot iron will melt monofilament thread – it doesn't!

Stained Glass Heart Wallhanging using the large Perfect Fit Heart and Clover Baby Blue ¼" Quick Bias. Embroidery designs by Husqvarna/Viking.

24. When all stitching is completed, square up the quilt. Please always take extra care on this step. If each corner of the wallhanging or quilt is square, the borders and binding will go on squarely and evenly – making your sewing life easier.

Binding The Wallhanging

The wallhanging can be bound with matching variegated Clover Border Bias. There is a variegated Border Bias to match each of the four variegated multi-colored Quick Biases. The Border Bias is ¾-inch wide, making the finished binding ⅜-inch wide.

25. Open the Border Bias up and remove the two papers that cover the fusing.

26. Pin the raw edge of one side of the Border Bias onto the wallhanging in the same way bias binding would be applied.

27. Sew Border Bias onto the quilt or wallhanging sewing in the first fold nearest raw edges.

28. When Border Bias is turned to the back, press miters in place. Press binding to back of wallhanging.

29. To finish binding, no pinning is needed. Hand stitch fused binding to back.

Helpful Hint: If bias does not fit there may be to much sizing in the fabric, wash the fabric.

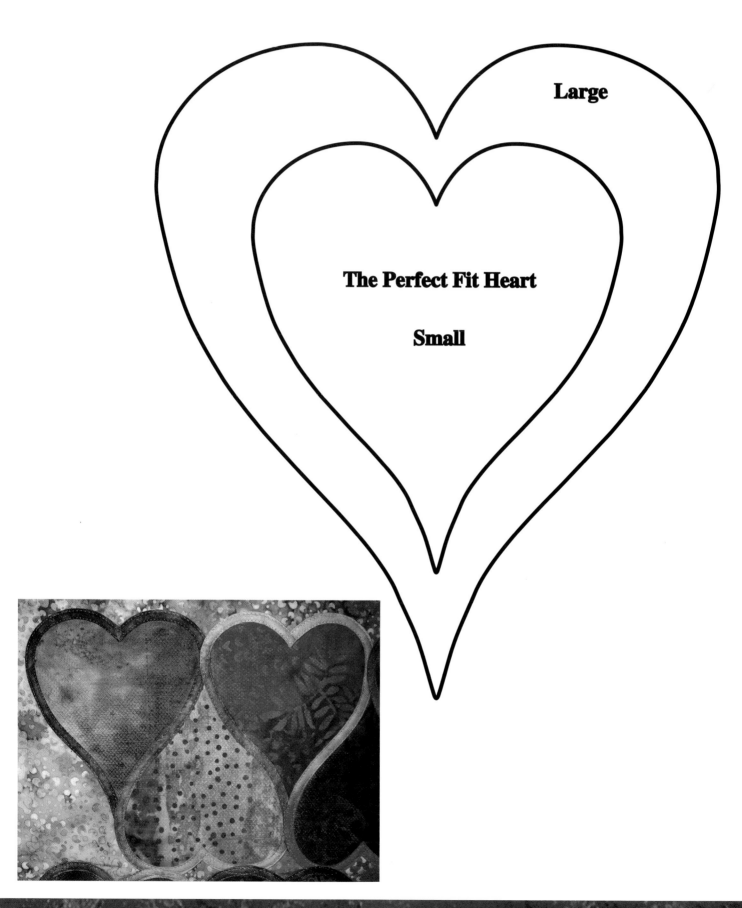

Large

The Perfect Fit Heart

Small

Stained Glass Pine Trees

Wallhanging 24½" x 25½"   Placemats 18½" x 12½"   Table Runner 51" x 12½"

This is a pattern for a wallhanging featuring just one fused pattern piece – a simple pine tree. The raw edges of the pine trees are finished with ¼-inch fusible bias applied continuously in rows for easy, non-stop machine sewing. There are no borders on this project which makes it quick to finish. Borders can be added, if desired.

See page 18 for QUICK OVERVIEW

Additional Materials Needed :
- 16 yards of metallic Clover Quick Bias for wallhanging; four yards for each placemat; 17 yards for table runner.
- Pre-washed, light-colored fabric: 27 inch square for wallhanging; 19½" x 13½" for placemat; 52" x 13½" for table runner.
- ¼ yard each of red and green fabric for wallhanging; ⅛ yard each for placemat; ½ yard each for table runner.

Prepare Background Fabric

1. Cut background fabric and red and green trees for the project selected. Over-The Mantle Wallhanging has four rows of trees including 14 full trees and four half trees; Placemat has two rows of trees including five full trees and two half trees; Table Runner has two long rows of trees including 15 full trees and two half trees.

> NOTE: Half the trees will be cut from green fabric and half from red fabric.
>
> One row is defined as a line of red and green trees right-side up and the upside-down trees of white fabric that fill in the tree shapes between the red and green trees. The white fabric is not actual cut tree shapes but just the tree shapes formed between the red and green trees.

2. Make sure background fabric is squared up. (There is an extra inch of background fabric to allow for squaring up when all sewing is completed.)

3. Mark a chalk line 1 inch down from the top raw edge horizontally across the background fabric and 1 inch in from left side vertically.

Preparing Pine Trees

4. Make a plastic template of Perfect Fit Pine Tree shape.

5. Carefully trace in pencil 14 trees and four half trees for wallhanging onto Lite Steam-A-Seam 2; or five trees and two half trees for placemat; or 15 full trees and two half trees for table runner. Leave a ¼ inch of space between trees on Lite Steam-a-Seam 2.

> HELPFUL HINT – If fabric needs to be fussy cut make a window template for tree cut as shown on page 78.

For cutting trees refer to page 79, steps 6–8.

Stained Glass Tree Layout

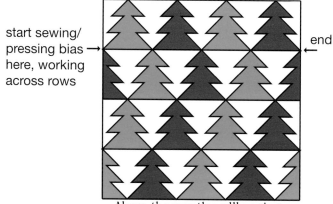

start sewing/ pressing bias here, working across rows → ← end

Above-the-mantle wallhanging

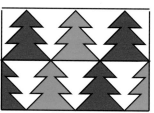

Placemat

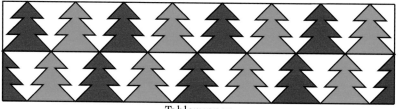

Tablerunner

9. Starting with top left tree, lay the first row of trees on background fabric from left to right. The first tree touches the top horizontal chalk line at its top and touches the left vertical chalk line on its left edge.

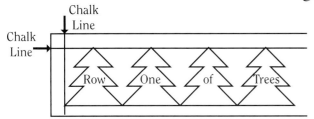

IMPORTANT -- Make sure widest bottom points of trees touch each other or slightly overlap.

10. Press first row of trees in place.

11. Lay the second row of Perfect Fit Trees under the first row, making sure the red and green trees are under the upside-down white trees from first row. Press these trees in place. Repeat for the remaining rows of trees.

12. Place the half trees at sides of project and press in place to complete pattern.

Press Bias To Trees in Continuous Rows
13. Turn the Clover Mini Iron to "high" and let it warm up about 10 minutes.

NOTE: The Clover Mini Iron is calibrated so as not to burn metallic Quick Bias. A regular iron set to a high setting can burn metallic bias.

14. Starting at the bottom point of the tree at the top left of the wallhanging, press bias along tree shape. Miter with a pleat at tree inward point and at tree branch points.

15. Continue fusing Quick Bias in place traveling up one side of colored-fabric tree and down the other making sure Quick Bias is sticking. If not, leave the iron on the Quick Bias longer.

16. After the sides of all trees are fused, press one straight line of bias across the bottom of each row of trees.

17. Fuse bias on all four sides of wallhanging, placemat or table runner.

Sew And Quilt In One Step
Refer to pages 80–81, steps 19–24.

Binding The Wallhanging
Projects can be bound with matching gold metallic Clover Border Bias. The Border Bias is ¾-inch wide, making the finished binding ⅜-inch wide.

Refer to page 81; steps 25–29.

Placemats and table runner can be finished with a ¼-inch wide bias edge in this way.

Square up placemat or table runner to exact finished size. Fuse bias to raw edge on all four sides by laying calculator tape paper under the fabric edge. Machine sew with the twin needle through the bias and through the paper. Tear paper away.

The Perfect Fit Tree

Stained Glass Pine Tree Placement

Sliced Pickles

Wallhanging 15" x 18"

The single, almond shape used in this pattern is one used in such historic quilt patterns as the Orange Peel, Robbing Peter To Pay Paul or Tea Leaf. This pattern is similar to all these patterns but what makes it different is the way the colors and shape form the pattern.

Materials Needed:
- Background fabric cut 15" x 18"
- Thin batting cut 16" x 19"
- Backing fabric cut 16" x 19"
- ½ yard of fusible web
- 4" x 2" piece of template plastic
- 8" x 4" piece of 7 fabrics. Choose

the 7 colors of the color wheel – yellow, orange, red, magenta, purple, blue and green to make a Rainbow wallhanging

- Seven yards of coordinating Clover ¾-inch wide Border Bias for binding
- Two spools of clear monofilament thread or matching polyester or cotton-covered polyester thread
- Clover Mini Iron
- Twin needle 2.5/90

1. Prewash then cut the background fabric 15 " x 18".

2. Trace 35 almond-shaped pieces onto the paper side of fusible web. Roughly cut out each piece and press them onto seven different fabrics. (Press five on each color.)

3. With the paper side facing toward you, cut the almond shape out exactly on the drawn line.

> NOTE: Take your time cutting – precision pays off.

4. Remove paper from the almond shapes.

5. On background fabric draw a chalk line 2¼ inches parallel to all four raw edges.

6. Lay the widest part of each almond-shaped patch on the chalk lines centering the patches as in the Layout Diagram on page 89.

> IMPORTANT
> Make sure patch points touch.

7. Press patches in place.

8. Begin at the START point on the diagram press the ⅛-inch wide fusible Mini Bias in place following the numbers on the Layout Diagram.

9. Do not cut the Mini Bias until arriving at the very end point which is the starting point. Cut the bias ⅜-inch longer than the ending point. Fold and tuck the raw edge under and press in place.

10. Layer backing, batting and quilt top.

11. Apply temporary fabric adhesive between the three layers of the quilt.

12. Begin at the START point on the Layout Diagram with a machine back tack. Follow the numbers and watch carefully so that both needles come down squarely onto the Mini Bias. (Have fun! There is no stopping the sewing until the end.)

13. Back tack again at the END point.

Bind The Wallhanging:
Refer to page 81 steps 25–29.

Sliced Pickles Layout

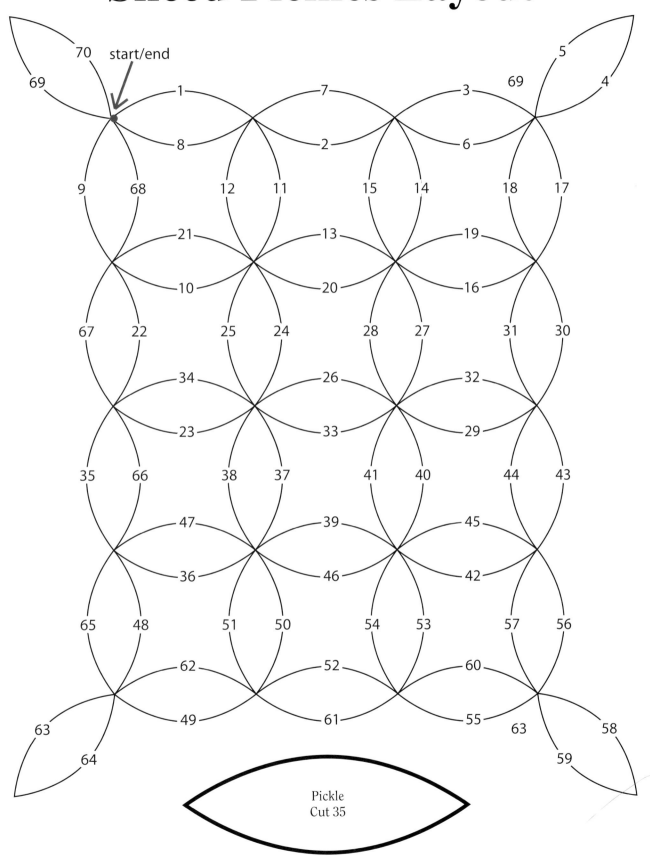

70   start/end
69

1
8
7
2
3
6

5
4
69

9   68
12   11
15   14
18   17

21
10
13
20
19
16

67   22
25   24
28   27
31   30

34
23
26
33
32
29

35   66
38   37
41   40
44   43

47
36
39
46
45
42

65   48
51   50
54   53
57   56

62
49
52
61
60
55

63
64
63
58
59

Pickle
Cut 35

Castle Window
Wallhanging 28" x 40"

Castle Window is a vision of an ornate stained glass window from an ancient castle. Through the stained glass window a colorful garden can be seen.

- Purple background fabric, cut 28" x 40"
- 22 yards (two spools) black ¼" Quick Bias
- ⅛ yd. green fabric for 36 small diamonds (B)
- ⅜ yd. pink fabric for 60 trapezoids (A)
- ½ yd. floral fabric for 25 lg. diamonds (C)
- ½ yd. batik yellow-green fabric for 4 arcs
- Four yards black ¾-inch Border Bias for binding
- Two spools black polyester or cotton thread
- Schmetz twin needle 4.0

1. Cut 36 small diamond (B) shapes from Lite Steam-A-Seam 2 and peel paper from back of each shape.

2. Press these 36 shapes onto the wrong side of green fabric and cut each shape out.

3. Repeat steps 1-3 for 60 trapezoid shapes cut from pink fabric, 25 large diamonds cut from floral fabric and four arcs cut from yellow-green batik fabric.

4. Peel backing paper from shapes. Lay shapes out as shown on top of background fabric. Raw edges must touch. There should be no spaces between pieces.

5. Press all pieces in place.

6. Continuously press black Quick Bias in place following the numbered order in Diagram 1.

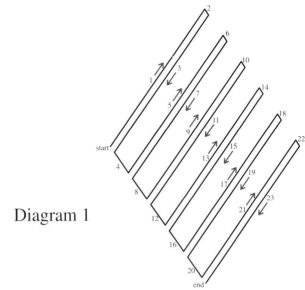

Diagram 1

7. Press 12 straight pieces of black Quick Bias following the numbered diagram below.

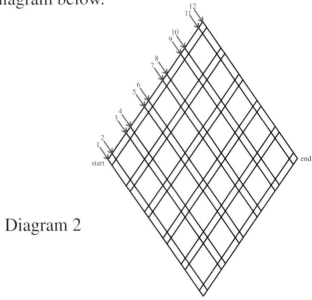

Diagram 2

8. Press black Quick Bias around outer edge of arcs.

9. Lay thin batting and backing fabric under Castle Window top. Apply spray adhesive between layers.

10. Twin needle stitch following the pressing sequence shown in the diagrams above.

11. Bind wallhanging with Border Bias.

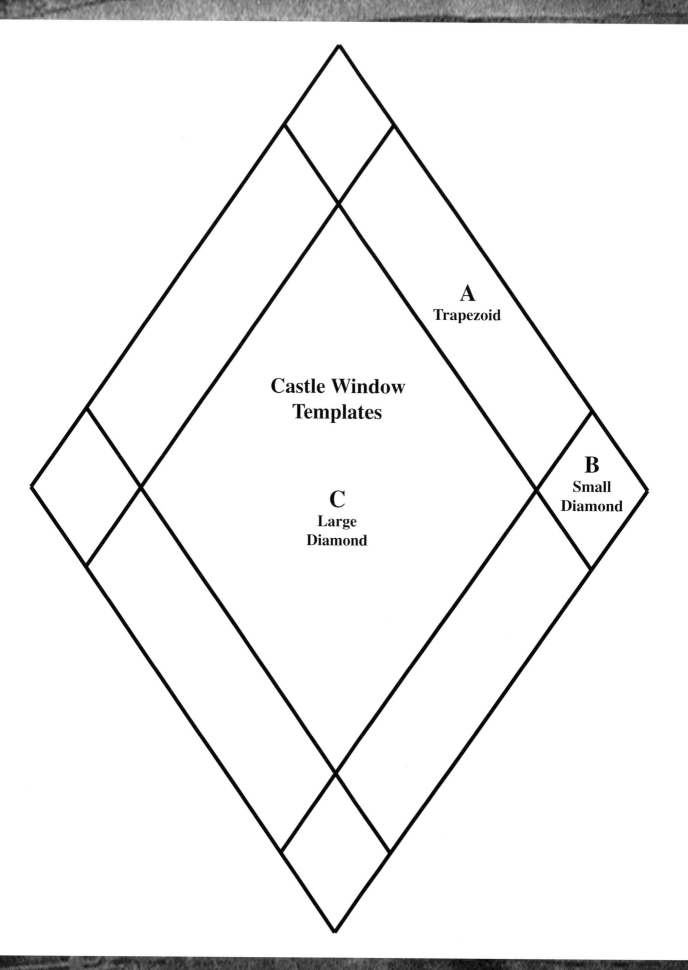

Castle Window
Templates

A
Trapezoid

B
Small
Diamond

C
Large
Diamond

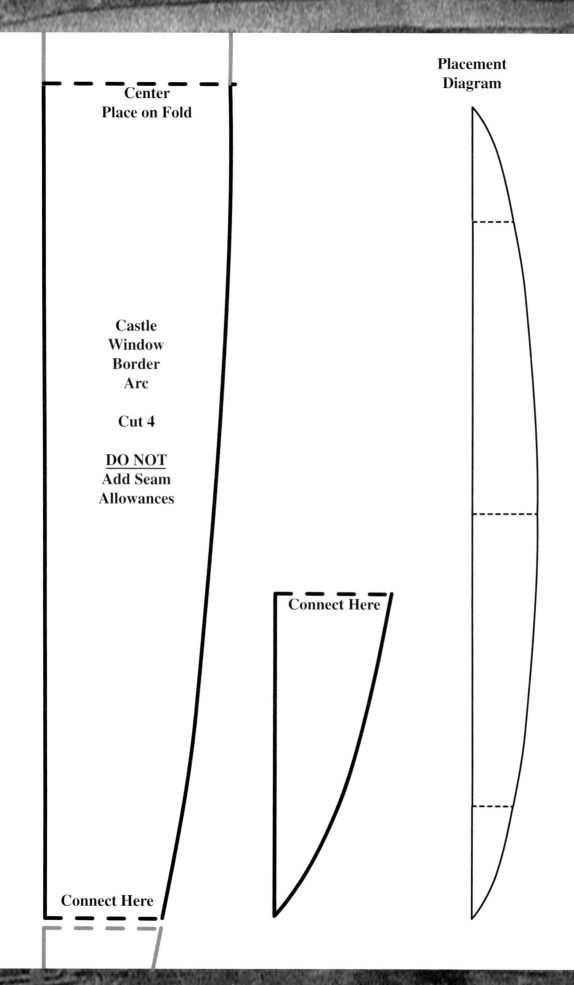

Center
Place on Fold

Castle
Window
Border
Arc

Cut 4

DO NOT
Add Seam
Allowances

Connect Here

Placement
Diagram

Connect Here

Daisy Potholder

Fabric and Clover Mini Bias Needed:
Cut a background fabric, batting and
   backing fabric each 7½ inches
Cut eight Daisy Petals and Daisy Center
One yard of Clover Rainbow Mini Bias.
One yard of Clover Rainbow Border Bias

1. Layer backing, batting and background
   fabric evenly. Apply spray adhesive.

2. Press Daisy Petals and Daisy Center at
   center of potholder.

3. Sew down Daisy flower as described
   previously for Dancing Daisy block.

4. Cut a three-inch piece of Border Bias and
   sew a loop into seam before attaching
   Border Bias on all four sides of potholder.

5. Open Border Bias strip up and lay one
   edge even with raw edges of potholder.

6. Sew in the fold on all sides of the
   potholder mitering corners.

7. Blindstitch Border Bias to back.

Between the Stitches with CindyO

Quilting and sewing are just plain fun. They have been favorite occupations of mine since I was seven years old.

Once when there was an illness in the family, I spent many an hour sitting in a hospital waiting room, as a nurse kept one eye on me because I was too young to go upstairs. I had to entertain myself, so there I sat with sewing projects from my Brownie troop and crocheting my aunt had taught me. That is where I learned to love working with my hands.

This is the gift we must pass on to our children. To work and to create with your hands is to occupy your mind and find peace. To create something from nothing is delightful. To give that creation to a loved one as a gift is a joy for the heart.

Creating and mixing color and playing with fabric is a never-ending pursuit. To discover that there are hundreds of thousands of others driven to create with their hands has been the best part of making sewing my job.

After 12 years, Quilter's Fancy is now an embellishment shop specializing in flowers in Cortland, Ohio, as well as a stop on the information highway. It has been a delight to design a shop filled with silk, French wire and other ribbons, charms, trims, silk scrap fabrics and unusual sewing notions.

My three earlier books on dimensional flowermaking from fabric and ribbon include *Into The Garden*, *The Enchanted Garden*, and *Dimensional Roses*. All are still available along with the tools required for each project, including The Ruching Edge, The Mini Ruching Edge and The Vintage Rose Spindle from Barbara Hall of Australia.

The best part of sewing is what happens between the stitches. This wonderful hobby brings all sorts of people together.

There can be two stitchers visiting the booth at a quilt show talking on and on like they have been best friends for years. You ask them how long they have known each other, and they say they only just met right there on the spot.

It was a great epiphany when I discovered that the unfinished projects are what we all have in common, but what really counts is what happens between the stitches.

Books, Tools & Supplies

All materials and tools including background fabric used in Flowers in a Flash are available from:

P.O. Box 457
800-484-7944 code 7673
Cortland, Ohio 44410
www.quiltersfancy.com

Call or write for a Free Catalog & Workshop Information

You are cordially invited to visit!

Visit the **Quilter's Fancy store of embellishments** at 130 N. High Street, Cortland, Ohio, 44410. Embellished silk fabric pieces, charms, silk ribbons, wire ribbons, beaded trims, cotton lame fabrics and fibers galore are our specialty for creating embellished fancywork such as crazy quilts, three-dimensional album quilts and silk ribbon embroideries.

Book and products available from Quilter's Fancy:

Video and DVD:

- Companion DVD & Video for Dimensional Roses & The Vintage Rose Spindle

Books & Companion Tools:

- Dimensional Roses For Quilts, Clothing & Accessories
- Vintage Rose Spindle by Barbara Hall, companion tool for Dimensional Roses
- Into The Garden, Realistic 3-D Flowers Faster By The Strip (also available in French)
- The Ruching Edge, companion tool to Into The Garden
- The Enchanted Garden, Miniature 3-D Flowers
- The Mini Ruching Edge, companion tool for The Enchanted Garden

Templates, Patterns & Notions:

- Victorian Ribbon Brooch Kit • Easy Gathered Bias Purse Kit
- 60 Leaves on Freezer Paper • All Clover Needlecraft Inc. products
- The 3-D Sunflower Kit & Pattern • The 3-D Pansy Kit & Pattern
- Full palette of french wire, Hanah silk, organza and silk ribbons
- Karisma Aquarelle Pencil, the quilter's favorite graphite pencil
- Charms, buttons, trims and silk fabric for crazy quilting & embellishing